Praise for the Pray for Me Campaign and Prayer Guide

I have long dreamed of a day when Christian parents and grandparents would not only *consider* the spiritual development of their children, but would also wholeheartedly *participate* in this grand endeavor. *Pray for Me* is an effective bridge for parents, grandparents, and others to begin the process of making next generation disciples of Jesus Christ.

Jack Eggar, President/CEO of Awana, Author of *Shaping Your Family's Faith*

Many churches and ministries have begun to awaken to the power and richness of intergenerational ministry, and yet implementation has been quite the challenge for the local church. The Pray for Me Campaign is one of the most exciting and practical ways of connecting the generations that I can think of. The greatest beauty is that this movement leans on the power of the Holy Spirit and not a program.

Nate Stratman, Pastor of Family Ministries at First Presbyterian Colorado Springs, Coauthor of *Building Your Volunteer Team*, Sticky Faith Coach, Ministry Architects Consultant

I am so excited about the Pray for Me Campaign. Tony has amazingly captured the importance of prayer in the life of the church and home. Every Christian should take advantage of these resources and create a prayer strategy for their ministry and family!

Ryan Frank, CEO and Publisher of KidzMatter

As a lifelong champion for children, I applaud Tony Souder's approach to an intentional prayer focus on individual, specific children that God has placed in our lives. The Pray for Me Campaign is a brilliant way to communicate a critical message to a child: "You matter! You are important to me and to God!" This unique tool is designed to spiritually impact the next generation of Christian leaders in a positive and profound way.

Dr. Wess Stafford, President Emeritus of Compassion International, Author of *Too Small to Ignore* **and** *Just a Minute*

Pray For Me

A PRAYER CHAMPION'S GUIDE
TO ESSENTIAL PRAYER FOR CHILDREN

Tony Souder

Read Avenue Press
CHATTANOOGA, TN

Tony Souder/Read Avenue Press
P.O. Box 2468
Chattanooga, Tennessee/37409
PrayforMeCampaign.com

Scripture quotations are from The Holy Bible, English Standard Version® (ESV®) Copyright © 2001 by Crossway, a publishing ministry of Good News Publishers. Used by permission.
All rights reserved.
ESV Text Edition: 2011

Book Layout ©2013 BookDesignTemplates.com

Cover Design by Nathan Mileur and Allison Dowlen

Pray for Me: A Prayer Champion's Guide to Essential Prayer for Children/ Tony Souder. —1st ed.
ISBN 978-0-9897545-6-9

Contents

To my daughters, Abby and Bethany:
You are treasured gifts from God, whose love and laughter remind
me often of His lavish goodness and favor.

"The LORD bless you and keep you; The LORD make his face to shine
upon you and be gracious to you; The LORD lift up his countenance
upon you and give you peace."

Numbers 6:24-26

Acknowledgements

First, I want to thank my wife, Rhonda, who has taught me more about enduring prayer and faith in Jesus than anyone else in my life. Like most parents I am indebted to my children, my twin daughters, Abby and Bethany, who have born the weight of my development as a parent over the years. Thank you!

Because this book is all about making a supernatural difference in the lives of children during their formative years, I want to give a special nod to all those who are called to serve children and families in the Church. Your role is vital and yet many times overlooked.

Writing a book is hard work and at least for me it would be an impossible feat if it were not for the stellar team God has raised up to make it a reality. Thank you to all the gracious friends who read, reflected, and helped make revisions that have resulted in a much better resource for the Body of Christ. Specifically I am thankful for the in-house *Pray for Me* team: Lauren Bozeman, Hannah White, Megan DeMoss, and Nathan Mileur. Thank you for your love for Jesus and your commitment to excellence. Outside of our incredible in-house team, God has been enormously gracious in bringing two new friends into my life, Brian Crowe and Deborah Addington, who have been instrumental in influencing me to write the Children's Edition of the Pray for Me Prayer Guide. Brian is a veteran AWANA missionary in Georgia and Deborah is a Children's minister with several decades of ministry experience investing in the lives of children and families. Their love for Jesus is contagious and their grasp of the benefits of the Pray for Me Campaign for children and youth is incredible. It was through a combination of conversations with Deborah and Brian that we decided to create the Children's Edition. Thank you for not holding back for the King and His Kingdom.

Lastly, I want to thank all those who have made it possible for the Pray for Me Campaign to launch across the nation. You know who you are; you are our financial partners, board, and staff members, both past and present. Thank you for believing in the importance of naturally creating relationships between generations through the catalyst of prayer. May God be praised and may each emerging generation know the sweetness of being deeply connected to the Body of Christ.

Preface

The Pray for Me Campaign is ultimately about the Church passing on the wonder and majesty of Jesus Christ to each emerging generation in a natural and sustainable way. It helps churches rally around families and builds a web of care and support that will sustain their children as they launch into adulthood. The importance of intergenerational connections in passing on a sustainable faith is hard to overstate. For over 50 years, Search Institute has been committed to learning the core factors that help a young person flourish. Their research revealed that young people who have at least three adults invested in their lives do far better in life.

For over a decade, The National Study of Youth and Religion has taken an in-depth look at the spiritual lives of American young people. This extensive study, along with the entire scope of Scripture, points to the indispensible role of adult believers in commending the greatness of God to the next generation Psalm 145:4 says, "One generation shall commend your works to another and shall declare your mighty acts." Psalm 71:17 and 18 say, "O God, from my youth you have taught me, and I still proclaim your wondrous deeds. So even to old age and gray hairs, O God, do not forsake me, until I proclaim your might to another generation, your power to all those to come." Both of these passages make it clear that adults are compelled to declare the greatness of God to the next generation. It seems that over the years, in spite of what we know to be true in Scripture and extensive national studies, we still have an incredibly difficult time motivating and empowering adult believers to effectively commend Jesus to young people.

The challenges facing youth today are formidable. It is imperative that we do everything we can to create strategic, natural, and spiritual bonds between adults and young people that will sustain them as they grow older. We believe this should begin in the formative years of childhood and continue to expand throughout adolescence. Our desire is that these crucial bonds will allow them to flourish in faith and life.

This is where the Pray for Me Campaign comes in. The Pray for Me Campaign is designed to get more adults caring for more children and teens more naturally than ever before. The plan is simply to help every child and teen connected to the Church to invite three adult believers from three different generations to become his or her Prayer Champions for a school year. Youth in grades six and above will personally invite the adults, whereas children in fifth grade and below will be assisted by parents or children's ministry leaders to find adults who will be their Prayer Champions. These Prayer Champions will pray using the Pray for Me Prayer Guide, which is designed specifically for the age of student they are praying for. The Prayer Guide empowers you as a Prayer Champion to pray effectively for your student during the entire school year through 7 Essential Biblical categories.

Why three adults from three different generations? The body of Christ is not limited to one age and every young person's team of Prayer Champions should reflect the body's scope—we believe that passing on a genuine faith is most effective when we can taste the sweetness of following Jesus from every generation.

The Pray for Me Campaign is a strategic step in mobilizing adults from every generation to intentionally begin investing in the lives of children and teens in a natural way. We have taken the most basic of Christian acts—prayer—and made it the connecting point between generations. Prayer not only establishes relationships across generational lines, it also creates a bond that is supernatural and lasting. May God be pleased in establishing relationships across generational lines throughout his entire Church. May our effectiveness in offering a clear picture of the beauty and majesty of Jesus to the next generation increase a hundredfold. Thank you for your role in this grand endeavor!

PRAY FOR ME CAMPAIGN OVERVIEW:

a simple way of investing in the next generation through prayer

ONE
FAMILY
INVITES

FROM
THREE
GENERATIONS

WHO ALL COMMIT TO
PRAYING
THROUGH THE GUIDE

THREE
ADULT BELIEVERS

TO BE THEIR KIDS'
PRAYER
CHAMPIONS

FOR ONE
ENTIRE SCHOOL YEAR

THE VISION: THAT EVERY YOUNG PERSON IN THE CHURCH WOULD HAVE A TEAM OF ADULT BELIEVERS SERVING AS THEIR PRAYER CHAMPIONS.

You may have this Prayer Guide in your hands because your church is launching the Pray for Me Campaign. Or, you may have come across this book on your own, and you are using it for your own personal prayer life. Regardless, the Prayer Guide is created to help empower individuals, and entire churches to invest in the next generation through prayer. If your church hasn't launched the campaign, perhaps you are the person to bring Pray for Me to them and help strengthen the intergenerational relationships within your church. Interested in learning more?

Visit our website: prayformecampaign.com

Before God enables his people to bring in a harvest, he pours out a Spirit of prayer upon them. The surest sign that God is about to send power upon us is a great movement of prayer in our midst.

—JOHN PIPER

Introduction: The Invitation

I was 17 when I accepted Christ as my Savior. I remember walking into church during those first few weeks after becoming a Christian. Adults repeatedly expressed their happiness for me, saying that they had been praying for me. As a newbie follower of Christ coming from a non-Christian home, I was clueless concerning the scope of what they were saying. When I reflect on what their prayers meant to me in those early days, several clear memories come to mind. First, I was shocked that I was on the radar of any of these people. After all, I was really a stranger to them. I was doubly surprised that they would take the time to pray for me. I also remember that surprise being swallowed up by a very strong sense of love and care from these adults. Their willingness to pray for me, and their expressions of care and concern, transformed the trajectory of my life. Though I was young, I did realize I had walked into a massive amount of goodness, and I liked it—a lot! The "goodness" that I had walked into was the Body of Christ, filled with people who knew God and wanted me to know him. God loves to use the private and public prayers of his people to change the world, to change a teenager's world, like mine.

It is likely that you are holding this book because you care about children and helping them flourish. You may have been invited by someone as part of the Pray for Me Campaign to serve as a Prayer Champion for a child. Being a Prayer Champion is a simple way to provide significant spiritual blessing and encouragement for the next generation. This book exists to help you fulfill your commitment to be their Prayer Champion. You may not feel like a Prayer Champion, but your acceptance of their invitation is a great affirmation that you are. This book will guide you in pleading God's provision, protection, and purposes to be established in the lives of those you pray for. When we begin to pray like this for others, something amazing happens inside of us as well. Our hearts become larger toward God and others. We begin to move toward others to bless and encourage them in ways beyond prayer. This book is designed with that in mind. Our hope is that you will find uncontainable joy in praying Scripture over this emerging generation. We also hope that you will respond with a resounding "Yes!" if and when God leads you to invest in their lives in other ways as well. We believe a wave of God's goodness will follow the prayers of his people. May the goodness of God begin to flow.

"Will you pray for me?" is such a simple request and yet it is too often not taken seriously enough. I would like to say that I have felt the full weight of each request when someone has asked me to pray for them, but that simply is not true. Regrettably, there have been times when I have not given the plea for prayer a second thought. Fortunately, my attentiveness to prayer was transformed one day when I was sitting in a hospital room after my wife's surgery in Long Island, New York. It wasn't like I was looking for transformation that day; I was minding my own business, reading through the Gospel of Matthew, when God opened my eyes to see a truth that in my blindness I had overlooked every other time I had read the familiar passage found in Matthew 7:7-12.

Ask and it will be given to you; seek, and you will find; knock, and it will be opened to you. For everyone who asks receives, and the one who seeks finds, and to the one who knocks it will be opened. Or which one of you, if his son asks him for bread, will give him a stone? Or if he asks for a fish, will give him a serpent? If you then, who are evil, know how to give good gifts to your children, how much more will your Father who is in heaven give good things to those who ask him! (Matthew 7:7-11)

I am very confident that you know the next verse, and yet, you may be surprised to find it here, in this context. It is the Golden Rule: "So whatever you wish that others would do to you, do also to them, for this is the Law and the Prophets" (Matthew 7:12).

Jesus put The Golden Rule right at the culminating point of a passage about deliberate, persistent, hopeful prayer. So here is my takeaway from that hospital room years ago: Jesus wants us to approach prayer for others with the same intensity and hopeful expectation as we would want them to approach praying for us. The Golden Rule can be used as a means to bring intensity and hopeful expectation to your prayers for others, especially your children, grandchildren, and the children and youth within our churches.

The Pray for Me Campaign is about hope, specifically the hope that young people can find in the greatness of God. Every generation needs to find their greatest hope, satisfaction, and enjoyment in God. This Campaign will help you lead children and teens to this hope through prayer. It is through prayer that the Holy Spirit sustains and strengthens our personal walk with God. This Prayer Guide is designed to help you and other adult believers call out to God for his loving provision, protection, and purposes in the lives of the next generation. The Campaign has three aims:

1. Help each emerging generation see and savor the greatness of God through the prayers of God's people.
2. Help adult believers be empowered as Prayer Champions who intentionally pray for and invest in the next generation.
3. Create a vast web of multi-generational relationships established by prayer, in which one generation would share the greatness of God with another.

Strategic Prayer

There are plenty of books out there about praying for others. What makes this one different? For starters, the prayers in this book are specifically geared towards children fifth grade and below. More importantly, this guide is designed to give your prayers focus, clarity, and consistency. There are three primary components whose combined uniqueness provide traction for this prayer guide:

- Praying the Scriptures
- The 7 Essentials
- SeeSavorShare (S3)

Praying the Scriptures

This prayer guide is rooted and established in the truths of Scripture. The Bible is the Word of God and as such has the power to give life to us and our prayers. Throughout this book you will learn how to turn Scripture into prayers for children. Praying Scripture is one of the most powerful and authoritative ways to pray. Let's take a moment to be reminded of some of the promises that await us as we soak in the Scriptures.

The Word of God:
- Gives life (Psalm 119:25, 107)
- Strengthens (Psalm 119:28)
- Guards from sin and keeps us pure (Psalm 119:9, 11)
- Creates and sustains the universe (Psalm 33:6, 2 Peter 3:5, Hebrews 1:3, 11:3)
- Creates spiritual life (1 Peter 1:23, James 1:18)
- Is able to save our souls (James 1:21)
- Is living and active and able to discern the thoughts and intentions of the heart (Hebrews 4:12)
- Produces faith (Romans 10:17)
- Teaches, reproves, corrects, and trains in righteousness (2 Timothy 3:16)

These passages offer a taste of the goodness that flows from the supremacy and power of the Word of God.

One of the compelling aspects about the Pray for Me Prayer Guide is that it takes the most powerful words in the world, the very words of God, and makes them the catalyst for our prayers for the next generation. The apostle Paul refers to the Scriptures as the Sword of the Spirit, and we know from Hebrews 4:12 that "the word of God is living and active, sharper than any two-edged sword, piercing to the division of soul and of spirit, of joints and of marrow, and discerning the thoughts and intentions of the heart." God uses his Word to transform our hearts whether it is written, spoken, or uttered silently in prayer to the Father. In this prayer guide I am committed to letting the very truths of Scripture be the fodder for our prayers. We will take passages of Scripture that relate to each of The 7 Essentials and turn them into life-giving prayers for children.

Praying like the Psalmist Prays

It would be hard to have a Scripture-centered prayer guide that didn't in some way point to the primary prayer and songbook in the Bible. Therefore, we will be taking cues from the Psalms in our efforts to turn Scriptures into prayers. They reveal a plethora of ways to plead with God. There is a grittiness and authenticity in the Psalms that promotes clarity, honesty, urgency, and directness. Let's look at a few phrases from Psalm 119 that can give us a glimpse into the psalmist's directness and dependence on God in prayer:

- Do good to your servant (17)
- Open my eyes that I may see (18)
- Remove from me scorn… (22)
- Preserve my life according to your word (25)
- Teach me your decrees (26)
- Let me understand the teaching of your precepts (27)
- Strengthen me (28)
- Keep me from deceitful ways (29)
- Do not let me be put to shame (31)
- Give me… (34)
- Direct me… (35)
- Turn my heart… (36)
- Turn my eyes… (37)
- Fulfill your promise… (38)
- Take away… (39)
- May your unfailing love… (41)

- Do not snatch your word from my mouth (43)
- Remember... (49)
- Be gracious (58)
- Let your compassion... (77)

Each of these phrases is a clear call for God to act; a plea for the favor of God to act on the psalmists' behalf. As we turn Scripture into prayer for children, we are ushering a clear call for God to act on their behalf. May God be ever so gracious to act and intervene for the good of the next generation! May he cause us to be relentless in our prayers and our intentionality in bringing his greatness to them. May God soften their hearts to his greatness and grant them faithful responsiveness to his Word and to us as Prayer Champions as we care for them.

The 7 Essentials

This prayer guide is structured around what I call the 7 Essentials. These seven aspects of life are the minimum essentials that I believe need to be attended to for someone to flourish in living faithfully before God and man.

The 7 Essentials come directly from two passages of the Bible, but their importance saturates all of Scripture. The first two, wisdom and favor, come from Luke 2:52: "And Jesus increased in wisdom and in stature and in favor with God and man." It is not surprising that Jesus grew in wisdom and favor because he was God in human form. What is surprising is that Luke makes sure that we know Jesus grew in wisdom and favor. Luke could have said anything he wanted about Jesus, but he made a point to let us know that wisdom and favor with God and man were essential, even for the Son of God. If it was essential for God's Son to grow in wisdom and favor, then there is no question that these two are essential for us. The other five Essentials are found in 1 Timothy 4:12: "Let no one despise you for your youth, but set the believers an example in speech, in conduct, in love, in faith, in purity." It is crucial to understand that Paul is not using throwaway words here. He is giving Timothy the essential categories that he needs to pay attention to in order to set an appropriate example for all believers. There was a lot at stake in this simple and precise directive from Paul to Timothy. These categories remain essential for us today.

In this prayer guide The 7 Essentials have been arranged into three categories based on the role of each Essential:

- The Favor Foundation: Favor
- The Core Four: Wisdom, Love, Faith, and Purity
- The Public Relations (PR) Pair: Speech and Conduct

The Favor Foundation

The One World Trade Center in New York City stands 1,776 feet tall, making it one of the tallest buildings in the Western Hemisphere. It's 408-foot spire graces the Manhattan skyline. As we marvel at the grandeur of such a structure, how often do we take time to consider its foundation? Foundations are easily forgotten and yet they are indispensible. Often times we forget that God's favor is the foundation of our lives. It is a strong and secure foundation, but in this world that values self-reliance, it is easy to forget that we are completely dependent on him. Think of God's favor as anything he does in, through, or for you. We can see the favor of God in his provision, protection, presence, and purposes.

He [Jesus] is the image of the invisible God, the firstborn of creation. For by Jesus all things were created, in heaven and on earth, visible and invisible, whether thrones or dominions or rulers or authorities— all things were created through Jesus and for Jesus. And Jesus is before all things, and in Jesus all things hold together. (Colossians 1:15-17)

Our entire existence results from God's creating and sustaining favor. This is the foundation for all the other Essentials. What does a child need to recognize God's favor in their lives? They need eyes to see, ears to hear, and humble hearts to understand and embrace the favor of God for all it is worth. We must be diligent in praying that the next generation of children develops a posture of humility so that they might see the favor of God in his provision, protection, presence, and purposes.

The Core Four

I call wisdom, love, faith, and purity the Core Four because they reflect the condition of our hearts. They represent the substance of who we are. It is in these areas that we need God to unleash his favor first and foremost. We need:

1. *Wisdom.* The children we are praying for are making decisions every day that will affect the rest of their lives. It is our desire that God would use our prayers to enhance their wisdom in order to make good decisions— and to reduce their regrets when they don't. We should look to the book of Proverbs and the person of Jesus as we pray for wisdom to take root in the next generation. Proverbs specifically seeks to provide "knowledge and discretion to the youth" (Proverbs 1:4). In Colossians 2:3, Paul says that "in [Jesus] are hidden all the treasures

of wisdom and knowledge." As we pray for these children's relationships with Jesus to deepen, we are also addressing their need for greater and greater wisdom.

2. *Love.* God is love. Love for God and others is the crux on which all the law and prophets hang according to Matthew 22:37-40:

> *And he said to him, "You shall love the Lord your God with all your heart and with all your soul and with all your mind. This is the great and first commandment. And a second is like it: You shall love your neighbor as yourself. On these two commandments depend all the Law and the Prophets."*

Love is what transforms us. That is why the apostle Paul was so intentional in Ephesians 3:18-19, praying that believers "may have strength to comprehend with all the saints what is the breadth and length and height and depth, and to know the love of Christ that surpasses knowledge, that you may be filled with all the fullness of God."

3. *Faith.* Faith is the gift of God's favor that makes salvation possible (Ephesians 2:8-9). Faith is absolutely necessary in pleasing God. Hebrews 11:6 says, "[W]ithout faith it is impossible to please him, for whoever would draw near to God must believe that he exists and that he rewards those who seek him."

4. *Purity.* Blessing and favor of God follow the pure in heart. God gives us vision to see him as we pursue a life of purity. Matthew 5:8 says, "Blessed are the pure in heart, for they shall see God." As we pray for these chil-

dren it is essential that we seek God's favor to cause their wisdom, love, faith, and purity to flourish.

The PR Pair: Speech and Conduct

I love watching the award-winning specials produced by National Geographic. The clarity of nature that they are able to capture is stunning. I am specifically reminded of a photograph of an iceberg in Pleneau Bay off Pleneau Island, which is close to the Antarctic Circle. The photograph was a split shot view capturing a unique image of the iceberg both above and below the waterline. It brought the phrase "tip of the iceberg" to life. Scientists state that because of the density of ice, only ten percent of an iceberg is visible above water, while the bulk of its substance sits below the surface. When you think about it, we are actually a lot like icebergs. People around us get to see about ten percent of who we really are through our speech and conduct—yet there is so much more to us that is "under the waterline." In some ways, our speech and conduct are like high-tech animated billboards above the surface sending messages to all who pass by saying, "This is who we are!" and "This is what we are made of!" Like all messages from billboards, our speech and conduct only serve as signs of who we are below the surface. They give clues, but they don't share the whole story. They are just the tip of the iceberg.

It is in our speech and conduct that we "go public" with who we are, or at least who we want people to *think* we are, on the inside. Our wisdom, love, faith, and purity are forged on the inside and then expressed on the outside in what we say and do. This is where the rubber meets the road in our Christian lives. The importance of our speech and conduct cannot be overstated. The goal is for what we say and do to accurately reflect who we are on the inside. It is through what we say and do that we offer the world a clear or hazy picture of God. We were created by God to magnify his greatness by our lips and by our lives.

I want to challenge you with two simple questions to help guide you in becoming an authentic follower of Christ in both your speech and conduct. These questions are designed to shine a light on the state of your hearts and to direct you toward an ever-increasing dependence on God.

1. *Am I playing the part without the heart?* God's greatest desire for us is that we would love him with all our heart, soul, mind, and strength, and that we would love others as ourselves. This question points to our propensity to pretend that he is our treasure when other things are our pleasure. Jesus saved some of his most scathing words for those who honored him with their lips while their hearts were far from him. Let this question do its good work and prompt us toward having a heart that is captured by God and his greatness.

2. *Am I allowing my speech and conduct to fulfill their purpose in my spiritual growth?* Our speech and conduct have several purposes—to communicate to the world who we are and what we stand for, and to communicate with ourselves. Are you listening to what your speech and conduct are telling you about the spiritual condition of your heart? As Christians, we have the Holy Spirit living in us and letting us know when we say or do something that is out of sync with either who we are or who God calls us to be. It is crucial that we listen to the Spirit's convictions and promptings. We must be

careful not to resist and quench the Holy Spirit's working within us. We must listen to the Holy Spirit when
he brings our sin and inconsistencies to light and respond by confessing and forsaking them by his power.
This is one of the key ways in which we are conformed
to the image of Jesus, which is God's ultimate purpose
for our lives.

The SeeSavorShare Discipleship Process

As you launch into this prayer guide, I want to introduce
you to a simple process that can help your walk with God flourish.
It is the SeeSavorShare (S3) discipleship process, which is the third
component that makes this prayer guide unique. Over the last decade S3 has become the rhythm of my life with God, and I would
like to encourage you to embrace it as your own as well. First, I
want to give a little background concerning the value and necessi-
ty of S3. I have been a follower of Christ since 1978, but in March
of 1995 God enrolled my wife and me in an intensive spiritual
growth course. It was at that time that my wife began having se-
vere migraine-like headaches. Over the next eighteen years, with
three major surgeries and fifty-plus doctors from all across the
country in our rearview mirror, her pain has not decreased but
expanded to include intense muscle and bone pain that has caused
countless tear-filled nights.

We have experienced the full spectrum of Western, East-
ern, conventional, and unconventional medical approaches. From
a Christian spiritual perspective we have experienced the full spectrum of biblical prayer and healing efforts on both individual and
corporate levels. It has been in this extended season of suffering
that I have had to learn to walk with God in a new way. Anyone

can live for God when the wind is at his or her back and all is well, but this was not my experience. I was constantly being called on to be more than I had capacity to fulfill, and the S3 discipleship process became, and still is, my spiritual survival process. Thankfully, you do not have to experience eighteen-plus years of suffering to begin seeing, savoring, and sharing the greatness of God that is all around you. You can begin the process today. S3 is the intentional process of looking for God in all of life. It is a thrilling way to walk with God and fuel a lavish love for him and others, regardless of your circumstances. It is God's desire for us to see his goodness, kindness, mercy, faithfulness, and love in all of life's situations. As he gives us a vision of his greatness in our lives, we must savor it for all it is worth with thanksgiving, praise, and adoration. It is out of the overflow of our savoring that we share freely with others daily. This process can send life deep into your soul, just as taking in oxygen brings life to the body. S3 can become the rhythm of your life with God.

At the very core of S3 are three powerful truths:

1. Everything God does is great, so everything we see about who God is, what he is doing, or has done should be savored and shared.
2. We can see the greatness of God in Scripture, our daily lives, and in all of creation.
3. The Bible is the only reliable source for understanding what is true about God and what he is doing in our lives and the world around us.

Seeing

Seeing the greatness of God is the first step. The greatness of his character and works can be seen all around us. It is God's desire that we see all of the various aspects of his greatness. He wants our hearts and minds to be captured by the magnificence of his holiness, justice, righteousness, power, wisdom, goodness, patience, kindness, faithfulness, gentleness, and love. His wonders are endless! If our relationship with God ever grows stale, it is not because he is not grand enough to capture the expanse of our hearts; it is because we are blind to the fullness of his beauty. Just as blind Bartimaeus diligently pursued Jesus to give him sight (Mark 10:46-52), so must we be intentional in asking God to give us spiritual sight to see his greatness all around us. Here are some things to remember about seeing God's greatness:

- We can see his greatness in Scripture, life, and creation.
- We can see, hear, and understand what he empowers us to, so one of our constant prayers must be for God to give us eyes to see, ears to hear, and hearts to understand his will and working in this world.

Savoring

Savoring the greatness of God that we see in Scripture, life, and creation is the next step of S3. Savoring is the heart's response to what we are seeing of God. Savoring is essential to our growth with God because it is about enjoying and delighting in God and his greatness. Savoring moves us away from simply having intellectual knowledge of God; it moves us closer to personally knowing him and what he cares about. It moves us closer because sustained savoring expands our heart's capacity to love God. Here are some things to remember about savoring God's greatness:

- Savoring is essential because we pursue what we love with purpose and intensity.
- Savoring takes time. We have to slow down and ponder what we have seen.
- Giving thanks, delighting, and treasuring are key aspects of savoring.
- Begin savoring by recalling times or places in your life where you have seen God's presence, protection, or provision.

Sharing

Sharing about God is the natural overflow of seeing and savoring his greatness. Sharing actually plays two primary roles for us in our growth with God. First, it completes the enjoyment of what we have seen and savored. When we see something incredible, we immediately begin looking for someone to share it with. Sharing is the culminating point in enjoying the greatness of God we have seen. Second, sharing helps us see what has a hold on our hearts. We naturally talk about what we love and enjoy. S3 is designed to help us deepen our love and enjoyment in God by seeing, savoring, and ultimately sharing his greatness with others. Here are a few things to remember about sharing God's greatness:

- Pay attention to what you talk about most. This can give you some insight into what holds the most space in your heart. The goal in this process is that you would begin to see and savor the greatness of God in your life, and sharing would naturally become the next step.

- To begin sharing, engage others about where they have seen God at work in their lives. Most people will have a time or place where they would say God has worked in their life.

- Be prepared to share stories about how you've seen God's greatness in your life. Sharing deepens your relationship with God in Christ. Philemon 6 says, "I pray that the sharing of your faith may become effective for the full knowledge of every good thing that is in us for the sake of Christ." This is a great encouragement and promise! This means every time we ask someone to share how God has worked in their lives, we are providing a means of establishing them in their faith. So don't hesitate to share, and don't hesitate to ask others to share!

S3 is included in this prayer guide to bring the abstract truth about God into the present reality of your life. When we pray for children, we must remember to pray with a vision of their being captured by the greatness of God. Each day we will pray one of The 7 Essentials using S3 as our lens to help provide focus and clarity for these prayers. May God grant us favor to see and savor his greatness in Scripture, life, and creation, so we will be ready to convey it to the next generation. Let's pray that God would unleash his favor in and through the next generation of children!

Make the Prayers Your Own!

As you begin your journey through the prayers in this guide, remember to make them your own! Each prayer is written in plural form to allow you ease in praying for several people at once. There will be a tendency to read through the prayers in a rote manner; resist this tendency. Hover over the words and phrases and soak in their meaning. Find freedom in expanding and enhancing the prayers as you offer them to God.

The 7 Essentials in 7 Days

Every day is designed to provide you with a clear and fresh opportunity for engaging God in Scripture through prayer for the child you are praying for. You'll notice, however, that each prayer is written in the plural tense so you can pray for more than one individual. It is our hope that you will pray for your student as well as anyone God may put on your heart.

The S3 life and ministry model guides you through each day, prompting you with ways to see, savor, and share the fullness of God. The *see* portion is a passage of Scripture where you can circle or underline words and phrases that stand out to you. Next, you will *savor* those truths in prayer for your child. Finally, you will have the opportunity to record any thoughts or ideas that were pressed into your heart during the see and savor portions. It is our hope and expectation that you will *share* them with someone else!

Day One: Favor

Father, open my eyes that I might *see* you more clearly, *savor* you more fully, and *share* you more freely.

Circle or underline any key words or phrases you *See:*

Yours, O LORD, is the greatness and the power and the glory and the victory and the majesty, for all that is in the heavens and in the earth is yours. Yours is the kingdom, O LORD, and you are exalted as head above all. Both riches and honor come from you, and you rule over all. In your hand are power and might, and in your hand it is to make great and to give strength to all. And now we thank you, our God, and praise your glorious name. (1 Chronicles 29:11-13)

Savor these truths in prayer:

Father, you are great and worthy to be praised. I pray that you would give your boundless favor to _____, so that they may have eyes to see your greatness, power, and glory in all creation. Awaken their hearts and minds to begin understanding your faithfulness in their lives as Lord over all things. When they look at the sky above, cause them to know the heavens are yours! When they look in the mirror, cause them to know that they are yours. Create in them an unceasing reliance on you and your provisions of favor each day. May they continually become more enthralled by your greatness, causing their hearts to overflow with thankfulness at every thought of you. For your glory and their good, in the sovereign name of Jesus, amen.

Write down any thoughts or ideas you may want to *Share:*

Day Two: Wisdom

Father, open my eyes that I might *see* you more clearly, *savor* you more fully, and *share* you more freely.

Circle or underline any key words or phrases you *See*:

So teach us to number our days that we may get a heart of wisdom. (Psalm 90:12)

O Lord, make me know my end and what is the measure of my days; let me know how fleeting I am! (Psalm 39:4)

Savor these truths in prayer:

Father, it is so easy for days and years to pass by before we realize they are gone. I pray that _____ would learn, even at their young age, the importance of a single day. Teach them to savor the moments of every day as special gifts from you. As they learn to number their days, cause their hearts and minds to overflow with your deep and practical wisdom. Cause them to grow into adults who love you and bless others because they understand your sustaining love in their lives. Help them to realize this life is fleeting and that there is no time to waste in helping others see and savor your greatness. Give them a long-term view of life so they can make wise short-term decisions. Remind them that it is in living for you that their lives become the most fulfilling. For your glory and their good, in Jesus' name, amen.

Write down any thoughts or ideas you may want to *Share*:

Day Three: Love

Father, open my eyes that I might *see* you more clearly, *savor* you more fully, and *share* you more freely.

Circle or underline any key words or phrases you *See*:

For God so loved the world, that he gave his only Son, that whoever believes in him should not perish but have eternal life. (John 3:16)

For while we were still weak, at the right time Christ died for the ungodly. For one will scarcely die for a righteous person—though perhaps for a good person one would dare even to die—but God shows his love for us in that while we were still sinners, Christ died for us. (Romans 5:6-8)

Savor these truths in prayer:

Father, thank you that the magnitude of your love is seen in the life, death, and resurrection of your Son, Jesus. I pray that you would give _____ eyes to see that your amazing love displayed in Jesus has overcome all the sin that has separated them from you as their creator. Help them to understand that your love for them in Jesus is a gift of grace and cannot be earned or deserved. Even as they are young give them a clear sense of what sin is and how it separates them from God and from others. Give them faith to trust in Jesus alone to restore their relationship with God. For your glory and their good, in Jesus' name, amen.

Write down any thoughts or ideas you may want to *Share*:

Day Four: Faith

Father, open my eyes that I might *see* you more clearly, *savor* you more fully, and *share* you more freely.

Circle or underline any key words or phrases you *See*:

Trust in the LORD with all your heart, and do not lean on your own understanding. In all your ways acknowledge him, and he will make straight your paths. (Proverbs 3:5-6)

Savor these truths in prayer:

Father, life is so often complex and confusing. I thank you for your promises that provide hope and clarity in the midst of life's complexity. Today I pray that _____ would place their trust in you. Help them learn to surrender their lives to you, knowing how much you love them. Empower them to fight the urge to rely on their own understanding more than they rely on you and your guidance. Make their hearts tender towards you and your purposes so that it becomes as natural as breathing for them to look to you in all their ways. Help them to recognize and acknowledge all of your provisions as they see you make their paths straight. You are their God! Help them treasure you today with every breath, and cause them to call others to treasure you with all of their hearts as well. For your glory and their good, in Jesus' name, amen.

Write down any thoughts or ideas you may want to *Share*:

Day Five: Purity

Father, open my eyes that I might *see* you more clearly, *savor* you more fully, and *share* you more freely.

Circle or underline any key words or phrases you *See*:

How can a young man keep his way pure? By guarding it according to your word. With my whole heart I seek you; let me not wander from your commandments! I have stored up your word in my heart, that I might not sin against you. (Psalm 119:9-11)

Savor these truths in prayer:

Father, in a world that disregards purity, the question of the psalmist is vital: "How can a young man [or woman] keep their way pure?" A wholehearted pursuit of you and your Word is the answer. I pray that _____ would taste the sweetness of Scripture and desire it with their whole hearts. Help them to believe that your Word is the Sword of the Spirit that can lead, guide, and empower them to pursue purity in every decision. Give them the desire and will to hide your Word in their hearts that they might not sin against you. Holy, holy, holy is the Lord God Almighty. In Jesus' name, amen.

Write down any thoughts or ideas you may want to *Share*:

Day Six: Speech

Father, open my eyes that I might *see* you more clearly, *savor* you more fully, and *share* you more freely.

Circle or underline any key words or phrases you *See*:

It is good to give to thanks to the LORD, to sing praises to your name, O Most High; to declare your steadfast love in the morning, and your faithfulness by night... (Psalm 92:1-2)

Savor these truths in prayer:

Father, I praise you today. You are great and glorious. Help _____ to use their words to give you thanks for all you are and all you do. Give them joy in you so that their hearts overflow with songs of praise to your name. Help them to have a growing awareness of your great love for them each morning. Give them the ability to recognize your faithfulness throughout each day. Help them learn to not only see your deep and abiding love and faithfulness, but to soak it in and savor each aspect of your goodness. May their seeing and savoring overflow into learning how to naturally share their thankfulness for your goodness. Give them mentors and models who can show them what it means to love and adore you with thankfulness and praise. For your glory and their good, in Jesus' name, amen.

Write down any thoughts or ideas you may want to *Share*:

Day Seven: Conduct

Father, open my eyes that I might *see* you more clearly, *savor* you more fully, and *share* you more freely.

Circle or underline any key words or phrases you *See*:

He has told you, O man, what is good; and what does the LORD require of you but to do justice, and to love kindness, and to walk humbly with your God? (Micah 6.8)

Savor these truths in prayer:

Father, thank you for telling us what is good in this life along with the things you require of us to honor your name. I pray that _____ would learn to love what you require of them even as children. Make their hearts tender and responsive to all of your commands to do justice, love kindness, and walk humbly with you all of their days. Awaken their hearts and minds to the needs for love and mercy all around them and give them the wisdom, abilities, and tenacious desire required to meet those needs. Give them eyes to see the world the way you see it and grant them courage to stand against injustice for your glory and the good of those being mistreated. As they seek to promote justice and to love kindness in this world, empower them to do it with humility before you and man. For your glory and their good, in Jesus' name, amen.

Write down any thoughts or ideas you may want to *Share*:

Notes

The 7 Essentials in 7 Days

By now you are getting into the rhythm of praying for your young friend. You have just prayed a week of the 7 Essentials over them. Only God knows the extent of goodness he is bringing their way because of your prayers. As you begin praying a second week for your child, remember to pay attention to what God brings to the forefront of your mind. I tend to see these prayers as "spark" prayers. God can use these prayers as a spark of his goodness to ignite a blaze of ongoing prayer for your friend and others throughout the day. Let any thoughts or ideas you may have prompt you to drill down deeper in prayer. It could be that at the end of each prayer you ask yourself.

What one thing would I add to this prayer?
Or:
What is today's takeaway thought for ongoing prayer?

Day One: Favor

Father, open my eyes that I might *see* you more clearly, *savor* you more fully, and *share* you more freely.

Circle or underline any key words or phrases you *See*:

For by grace you have been saved through faith. And this is not your own doing; it is the gift of God, not a result of works, so that no one may boast. For we are his workmanship, created in Christ Jesus for good works, which God prepared beforehand, that we should walk in them. (Ephesians 2:8-10)

Savor these truths in prayer:

Father, thank you that salvation is a gift. Thank you that it is not based on our good works, but on Jesus' perfect work on the cross. I pray that you would give _____ faith to trust you alone for their salvation. Give them your abiding peace that comes from knowing your unconditional acceptance, which you displayed in Jesus' death, burial, and resurrection. Cause them to know how amazingly special they are as your workmanship. Help them to understand and pursue the unique purposes you have prepared for them as your children in Christ. Cause their good works to be a result of their relationship with you, not a means to gain a relationship with you. For your glory and their good, in the precious name of Christ, amen.

Write down any thoughts or ideas you may want to *Share*:

Day Two: Wisdom

Father, open my eyes that I might *see* you more clearly, *savor* you more fully, and *share* you more freely.

Circle or underline any key words or phrases you *See*:

And he said to man, "Behold, the fear of the Lord, that is wisdom, and to turn away from evil is understanding." (Job 28:28)

The fear of the Lord is the beginning of wisdom; all those who practice it have a good understanding. His praise endures forever! (Psalm 111:10)

Savor these truths in prayer:

Father, you are wise and wonderful in all you are and do. I pray today that _____ would fear you in a way that matches your worth. Cause them to see you and themselves accurately, which produces in them a fear of you that is full of deep respect, honor, and adoration. Create in them a humble dependence on you for all things. Give them deep satisfaction and joy in turning away from evil in both small and big things. Cause their hearts to be filled with insight and understanding concerning the pursuit of the paths of righteousness. Remove the obstacles that blind and deceive them from recognizing your perfect and sovereign work in this world. Make their hearts overflow with praise and thankfulness for all your goodness in their lives. Strengthen them in their ability to help others see your greatness. For your glory and their good, in Jesus' all-wise and wonderful name, amen.

Write down any thoughts or ideas you may want to *Share*:

Day Three: Love

Father, open my eyes that I might *see* you more clearly, *savor* you more fully, and *share* you more freely.

Circle or underline any key words or phrases you *See*:

And he said to him, "You shall love the Lord your God with all your heart and with all your soul and with all your mind. This is the great and first commandment. And a second is like it: You shall love your neighbor as yourself. On these two commandments depend all the Law and the Prophets." (Matthew 22:37-40)

Savor these truths in prayer:

Father, thank you that your greatest command is for our greatest good. I pray that _____ would seek to love you with all of their heart, soul, and mind. Establish yourself as the love of their lives even now in these formative years. Help them to learn to make decisions in their lives based on the supremacy of your love. Cause them to grow in their ability to know when they are beginning to love other things more than they love you. Give them understanding that their deepest desires can only be satisfied by loving you in all they say, think, and do. Give them an incredible desire and will to love others as they love themselves. Help them to have a keen sensitivity to the needs of those around them and a willingness to meet these needs. Let their lives be a constant demonstration of your love to the world. For your glory and their good, in the wonderful name of Jesus, amen.

Write down any thoughts or ideas you may want to *Share*:

Day Four: Faith

Father, open my eyes that I might *see* you more clearly, *savor* you more fully, and *share* you more freely.

Circle or underline any key words or phrases you *See*:

I know that you can do all things, and that no purpose of yours can be thwarted (Job 42:2)

Ah, Lord GOD! It is you who have made the heavens and the earth by your great power and by your outstretched arm! Nothing is too hard for you... "Behold, I am the LORD, the God of all flesh. Is anything too hard for me?" (Jeremiah 32:17, 27)

Savor these truths in prayer:

Father, life is filled with challenges and limitations that whisper and sometimes even shout at us saying we are not enough, and yet we rest in knowing that you are more than enough for everything we face in this life. I pray for _____ today, that you would give them faith in your ability to do all things. Help them to believe that there is no purpose of yours that can be thwarted. Help them learn the great stories in your Word that show your faithfulness in difficult times. When they face difficult times, remind them that nothing is too hard for you. Help them to learn the truth that you work everything for the good of those who love you, so that they might be conformed into the image of your Son. May you be praised forever! In Jesus' name, amen.

Write down any thoughts or ideas you may want to *Share*:

Day Five: Purity

Father, open my eyes that I might *see* you more clearly, *savor* you more fully, and *share* you more freely.

Circle or underline any key words or phrases you *See*:

I have made a covenant with my eyes; how then could I gaze at a virgin? (Job 31:1)

Sheol and Abaddon are never satisfied, and never satisfied are the eyes of man. (Proverbs 27:20)

Savor these truths in prayer:

Father, as I pray for _____ and their purity today, I ask that you would make them alert to the people, places, and things that they look upon. Help them to be like Job and make a covenant with their eyes, guarding their gaze and not looking at others inappropriately. Help them to diligently seek purity. Help them to understand that their purity can be fueled or foiled by the direction of their gaze. Protect them from the futility of trying to be satisfied by what they see. The eyes of man cannot be satisfied apart from you. You alone can create in them a satisfaction that supersedes all other lures or lusts that come before their eyes. For your glory and their good, in Jesus' name, amen.

Write down any thoughts or ideas you may want to *Share*:

Day Six: Speech

Father, open my eyes that I might *see* you more clearly, *savor* you more fully, and *share* you more freely.

Circle or underline any key words or phrases you *See*:

When words are many, transgression is not lacking, but whoever restrains his lips is prudent. (Proverbs 10:19)

There is one whose rash words are like sword thrusts, but the tongue of the wise brings healing. Truthful lips endure forever, but a lying tongue is but for a moment. (Proverbs 12:18-19)

Savor these truths in prayer:

Father, thank you for giving the gift of language and the ability to express ourselves with words. I pray you would bless _____ with your wisdom and favor so they can learn to use their words well. Give them wisdom on when to speak and when to keep silent. Protect them from being reckless with their speech and using rash words that damage and destroy. Give them courage to stand up for those who are being verbally bullied. Cause them to grow in your wisdom so that their words would bring healing everywhere they go. Give them a courageous commitment even as children to always speak the truth in love. Help them to observe in the world around them that a lying tongue always comes to an undesirable end. Cause them to be known for the kindness and encouragement in their words. For your glory and their good. In Jesus' name, amen.

Write down any thoughts or ideas you may want to *Share*:

Day Seven: Conduct

Father, open my eyes that I might *see* you more clearly, *savor* you more fully, and *share* you more freely.

Circle or underline any key words or phrases you *See*:

"This Book of the Law shall not depart from your mouth, but you shall meditate on it day and night, so that you may be careful to do according to all that is written in it. For then you will make your way prosperous, and then you will have good success. Have I not commanded you? Be strong and courageous. Do not be frightened, and do not be dismayed, for the LORD your God is with you wherever you go." (Joshua 1:8-9)

Savor these truths in prayer:

Father, I praise you and thank you for the promises in your Word. I pray that _____ would take hold of your Word with all their hearts and minds. Give them a craving for your Word, even as children, that causes them to read, memorize, and meditate on it day and night. Cause them to care about all that you command and be quick to obey you out of a heart of love for you, knowing your promises of goodness will follow. Create in them a courageous and strong resolve to pursue all that you desire for them. Don't let fear cause them to falter. Fill them with faith to believe they can follow you anywhere you command. Give them a sense of your powerful presence to strengthen them to pursue your purposes with courage. For your glory and their good, in Jesus' name, amen.

Write down any thoughts or ideas you may want to *Share*:

Notes

CONGRATULATIONS!

You've made it through your first two weeks of prayer! I hope you're enjoying the journey so far. Your prayers are making a lasting impact on the next generation.

The Pray for Me Campaign team would love to hear how it's going so far! Connect with us on social media to share your story of what God is doing and read stories from other Prayer Champions and students. You can also email us or chat with us on our website. We can't wait to hear from you!

www.prayformecampaign.com
info@theyouthnetwork.org

The Pray for Me Campaign

pfmcampaign

pfmcampaign

WEEK THREE

The 7 Essentials in 7 Days

rant me, O Lord my God, a mind to know you, a heart to seek you, wisdom to find you, conduct pleasing to you, faithful perseverance in waiting for you, and a hope of finally embracing you. Amen.
— ST. THOMAS AQUINAS

…a spiritual life without prayer is like the gospel without Christ.
— HENRI J.M. NOUWEN

Prayer is an act of brave trust in God. — RHONDA SOUDER

Day One: Favor

Father, open my eyes that I might *see* you more clearly, *savor* you more fully, and *share* you more freely.

Circle or underline any key words or phrases you *See*:

Let not steadfast love and faithfulness forsake you; bind them around your neck; write them on the tablet of your heart. So you will find favor and good success in the sight of God and man. (Proverbs 3:3-4)

Savor these truths in prayer:

Father, I pray for _____, that you would lavish them with your favor today. Help them to sense your steadfast love and faithfulness as they go about their day. Cause them to see your goodness and how you have loved and cared for them. Give them opportunities so they can help others know and experience your love and faithfulness today. May their lives be so clearly marked by your love and faithfulness that favor and success would be their constant companions. Cause them to feel your hand of favor on their lives and remind them that where they go, your favor goes with them. For your glory and their good, in Jesus' name, amen.

Write down any thoughts or ideas you may want to *Share*:

Day Two: Wisdom

Father, open my eyes that I might *see* you more clearly, *savor* you more fully, and *share* you more freely.

Circle or underline any key words or phrases you *See*:

For the LORD gives wisdom; from his mouth come knowledge and understanding; he stores up sound wisdom for the upright (Proverbs 2:6-7)

Blessed is the one who finds wisdom, and the one who gets understanding... (Proverbs 3:13)

Savor these truths in prayer:

Father, I pray that you would create in _____ a longing for you and your wisdom. I pray that you would give them eyes to see, ears to hear, and hearts to understand the wisdom found in your Word! Protect them from becoming foolish and proud and from not understanding the truth of how limited their knowledge and understanding really is. Cause them to humbly treasure the truth of your wisdom. Bless them in their relationship with you as they taste the sweetness of your wisdom. Create in them a deep understanding about life even as children, which enables them to be fountains of wise counsel to their friends. Make sharing about you and your wisdom as natural as breathing. For your glory and their good, in Jesus' name, amen.

Write down any thoughts or ideas you may want to *Share*:

Day Three: Love

Father, open my eyes that I might *see* you more clearly, *savor* you more fully, and *share* you more freely.

Circle or underline any key words or phrases you *See*:

For as high as the heavens are above the earth, so great is his steadfast love toward those who fear him; as far as the east is from the west, so far does he remove our transgressions from us. (Psalm 103:11-12)

Savor these truths in prayer:

Father, I pray that _____ would gain an ever-growing understanding that your love is great toward those who fear you! Stir up within them a sense of awe and respect for you that is unquenchable. Cause them to feel the bigness of your love for them that stretches to the highest heavens as they look at the daytime sky and the night's starry host. Thank you that your love and forgiveness are perfect and complete. Let them feel the freedom of your complete and unending forgiveness through Jesus and his sacrifice every single day. Help me to be open and available to show your love and forgiveness in any way that I can. For your glory and their good, in Jesus' name, amen.

Write down any thoughts or ideas you may want to *Share*:

Day Four: Faith

Father, open my eyes that I might *see* you more clearly, *savor* you more fully, and *share* you more freely.

Circle or underline any key words or phrases you *See*:

And those who know your name put their trust in you, for you, O LORD, have not forsaken those who seek you (Psalm 9:10)

Some trust in chariots and some in horses, but we trust in the name of the LORD our God. (Psalm 20:7)

Savor these truths in prayer:

Father, thank you for all of your promises in your Word. They are gifts to your children waiting to be unwrapped to unleash your faithfulness in our lives. I pray for _____, that they would know your character, causing their hearts to grow strong in faith and trust in your promises. Create in them confidence that your name represents all authority, power, and greatness. Help their hearts to be receptive to you as their Creator, Sustainer, Provider, Healer, and Redeemer. Help them to feel secure and safe in knowing that you will never forsake them. You are the Prince of Peace, so anoint them with your perfect peace. You are the King of Kings, so reign over them in all of your goodness. You are the Great I Am, so give them faith to trust you for all they need. For your glory and their good, in Jesus' name, amen.

Write down any thoughts or ideas you may want to *Share*:

Day Five: Purity

Father, open my eyes that I might *see* you more clearly, *savor* you more fully, and *share* you more freely.

Circle or underline any key words or phrases you *See*:

Blessed are the pure in heart, for they shall see God.
(Matthew 5:8)

Savor these truths in prayer:

Father, thank you for this day that you have ordained for _____. I pray for their happiness today. Jesus said that blessed are the pure in heart for they shall see God. Give them uncontainable joy in you. Don't let them miss the wonder and joy of seeing you because they settled for some false promise of pleasure elsewhere. Give them a magnificent vision of your greatness so that those empty promises would be powerless in their hearts. It is by your Spirit that they are empowered to walk in purity. Fill them with your Spirit today. Cause the joy from seeing your magnificence to overflow in blessing and purity to those around them. For your glory and their good, in Jesus' name, amen.

Write down any thoughts or ideas you may want to *Share*:

Day Six: Speech

Father, open my eyes that I might *see* you more clearly, *savor* you more fully, and *share* you more freely.

Circle or underline any key words or phrases you *See*:

The wise of heart is called discerning, and sweetness of speech increases per-suasiveness. Good sense is a foundation of life to him who has it, but the instruc-tion of fools is folly. The heart of the wise makes his speech judicious and adds persuasiveness to his lips. Gracious words are like a honeycomb, sweetness to the soul and health to the body. (Proverbs 16:21-24)

Savor these truths in prayer:

Father, thank you that your word tells us that out of the heart the mouth speaks and that a wise heart guides our speech to make a difference for good. I pray that _____ would have hearts that are being fueled by your wisdom so that their speech would be sweet and persuasive. May your hand of favor be so clearly on their lives that their speech powerfully discerning even for children. Help them to have friends who also have hearts that are rooted in wisdom so that they can encourage and correct each other along the way. Grant that their words would be filled with grace so that they would give comfort to the soul and body. For your glory and their good, in Jesus' name, amen.

Write down any thoughts or ideas you may want to *Share*:

Day Seven: Conduct

Father, open my eyes that I might *see* you more clearly, *savor* you more fully, and *share* you more freely.

Circle or underline any key words or phrases you *See*:

Good and upright is the LORD; therefore he instructs sinners in the way. He leads the humble in what is right, and teaches the humble his way. All the paths of the LORD are steadfast love and faithfulness, for those who keep his covenant and his testimonies. (Psalm 25:8-10)

Savor these truths in prayer:

Father, thank you that you are good and upright in all you do. Thank you that you correct us when we stray from your truth and instruct us in the way that we should go. I pray that you would create in _____ humble hearts that are teachable and responsive to all of your instruction and purposes. Help them understand that you lead the humble in all that is right and that you teach them to live in your ways. Give them a clear sense of joy in obeying your Word that flows from a growing conviction that all your paths are paved with steadfast love and faithfulness. Cause them to be relentless in pursuing your paths of steadfast love and faithfulness. Help them to make friends who help them in their pursuit of your purposes. Make your truth their treasure. For your glory and their good, in Jesus' name, amen.

Write down any thoughts or ideas you may want to *Share*:

Notes

The 7 Essentials in 7 Days

My daughter jokes about how she loves to run short distances at a long distance pace. I laugh every time she says it because I identify with it so much. I wonder if we could benefit by applying my daughter's running approach to our prayers. Here is what I mean: Even though they are short prayers, it doesn't mean you should speed through them. Pace yourself. You can even think of it as a prayer stroll. As you are praying, find a word, phrase, or sentence and linger over it for a little while. Don't feel the need to rush to the next sentence. Let God help you savor the elements of each passage and prayer long into the day. Enjoy your stroll.

Day One: Favor

Father, open my eyes that I might *see* you more clearly, *savor* you more fully, and *share* you more freely.

Circle or underline any key words or phrases you *See*:

What do you have that you did not receive? If then you received it, why do you boast as if you did not receive it? (1 Corinthians 4:7)

...since he himself gives to all mankind life and breath and everything... "in him we live and move and have our being." (Acts 17:25, 28)

Savor these truths in prayer:

Father, every breath is a gift of your grace and favor. I thank you for _____ today, and for giving them life and breath and all things. Show them your sustaining favor that makes it possible for them to live and move and have their being while playing, exploring and learning. Keep them from taking your enduring goodness and favor for granted. Give them eyes to see your sustaining favor and create genuine delight in their hearts today for each breath. Make their hearts full with thanksgiving for the gift of your gracious favor. For your glory and their good, in the all-sustaining name of Jesus, amen.

Write down any thoughts or ideas you may want to *Share*:

Day Two: Wisdom

Father, open my eyes that I might *see* you more clearly, *savor* you more fully, and *share* you more freely.

Circle or underline any key words or phrases you *See*:

The words of the wise are like goads, and like nails firmly fixed are the collected sayings; they are given by one Shepherd. My son, beware of anything beyond these. Of making many books there is no end, and much study is a weariness of the flesh. The end of the matter; all has been heard. Fear God and keep his commandments, for this is the whole duty of man. For God will bring every deed into judgment, with every secret thing, whether good or evil. (Ecclesiastes 12:11-14)

Savor these truths in prayer:

Father, thank you for reminding us that wisdom comes from you, the Great Shepherd. I pray that _____ would have an exceptional desire to want to know first and foremost what you think and say in your Word about how they should live. Help them wade deeply into the Biblical proverbs and the parables of Jesus, letting the truths soak thoroughly into their lives. Cause their understanding of life and how it works to grow deep and wide so that they would become incredible influencers for your purposes in this world. Strengthen them by the power of your Spirit to honor and obey you in all things, knowing that they're ultimately accountable to you. For your glory and their good, in Jesus' name, amen.

Write down any thoughts or ideas you may want to *Share*:

Day Three: Love

Father, open my eyes that I might *see* you more clearly, *savor* you more fully, and *share* you more freely.

Circle or underline any key words or phrases you *See*:

For the love of money is a root of all kinds of evils. It is through this craving that some have wandered away from the faith and pierced themselves with many pangs. (1 Timothy 6:10)

Keep your life free from love of money, and be content with what you have, for he has said, "I will never leave you nor forsake you." So we can confidently say, "The Lord is my helper; I will not fear; what can man do to me?" (Hebrews 13:5-6)

Savor these truths in prayer:

Father, as I pray for _____ today, I long for them to have their hearts captured by you and your love. So many things can steal their affections—the love of money being one of the most significant and potentially tragic. Your Word says that the love of money is the root of all kinds of evils. Protect them from ever allowing the love of money and all the material things it can buy to be the driving force of their lives. Help them understand that money provides a sense of security, which can tempt them to hope in money rather than your loving relationship with them. Give them confidence that you are their helper; there is no need to fear because you will never leave or forsake them. For your glory and their good, in Jesus' name, amen.

Write down any thoughts or ideas you may want to *Share*:

Day Four: Faith

Father, open my eyes that I might *see* you more clearly, *savor* you more fully, and *share* you more freely.

Circle or underline any key words or phrases you *See*:

The fear of man lays a snare, but whoever trusts in the Lord is safe. (Proverbs 29:25)

Savor these truths in prayer:

Father, I praise you today that you are great and glorious and worthy of all our trust. We do not need to be afraid and yet fear so often grips our hearts. I pray that you would help _____ to see your trustworthiness and learn to rest in your goodness. Help them not to be afraid of what man thinks of them. Cause them to know at an early age that being afraid of man only brings trouble, creating a snare in their hearts and minds. Set them free from those snares and limitations that come from giving man too big of a place in their hearts and minds. Cause their hearts to grow big in believing that you are safe and good and that you alone can set them free from the fear of man. Cause their trust in you to guide what they think, say, and do today. For your glory and their good, in Jesus' name, amen.

Write down any thoughts or ideas you may want to *Share*:

Day Five: Purity

Father, open my eyes that I might *see* you more clearly, *savor* you more fully, and *share* you more freely.

Circle or underline any key words or phrases you *See*:

Keep your heart with all vigilance, for from it flow the springs of life. (*Proverbs 4:23*)

And he said, "What comes out of a person is what defiles him. For from within, out of the heart of man, come evil thoughts, sexual immorality, theft, murder, adultery, coveting, wickedness, deceit, sensuality, envy, slander, pride, foolishness. All these evil things come from within, and they defile a person." (*Mark 7:20-23*)

Savor these truths in prayer:

Father, in our pursuit of following you in faithfulness and becoming like you in holiness, we realize that some actions are more important than others. Guarding our hearts is one of those vital acts. I pray that _____ would exercise vigilance in guarding their heart by the power of your Spirit. Help them to see the places where they need to protect their heart better. Help them to find friends that will strengthen their resolve to guard their hearts. Cause them to see with clarity the disappointing consequences of people who live with unguarded hearts. Fill them with your Spirit so that rivers of living water will flow out of them. For your glory and their good, in Jesus' name, amen.

Write down any thoughts or ideas you may want to *Share*:

Day Six: Speech

Father, open my eyes that I might *see* you more clearly, *savor* you more fully, and *share* you more freely.

Circle or underline any key words or phrases you *See*:

A soft answer turns away wrath, but a harsh word stirs up anger. The tongue of the wise commends knowledge, but the mouths of fools pour out folly...A gentle tongue is a tree of life, but perverseness in it breaks the spirit. (Proverbs 15:1-2, 4)

Savor these truths in prayer:

Father, thank you for the power of soft and gentle speech. I pray that you would provide _____ with people who would lavish them with the goodness of soft and gentle speech. In the same way I pray that they would be generous in offering up words that are soft and gentle to others. Cause the fruit of their words to be a tree of life, turning away wrath and anger. Let wisdom flow from their lips, commending knowledge that is life-giving to all who hear. Protect them from giving or receiving harsh words that stir up anger or hate. Give them the ability to graciously change the subject when perverse speech breaks out around them. Do not let evil and harsh words be used to harm them in any way. Help them to embrace your truth so they can overcome any false words directed toward them. For your glory and their good, in Jesus' name, amen.

Write down any thoughts or ideas you may want to *Share*:

Day Seven: Conduct

Father, open my eyes that I might *see* you more clearly, *savor* you more fully, and *share* you more freely.

Circle or underline any key words or phrases you *See*:

Be appalled, O heavens, at this; be shocked, be utterly desolate, declares the LORD, for my people have committed two evils: they have forsaken me, the fountain of living waters, and hewed out cisterns for themselves, broken cisterns that can hold no water. (Jeremiah 2:12-13)

Savor these truths in prayer:

Father, thank you that you are the fountain of living waters and the only place we can be perfectly satisfied. I pray that _____ would believe fully that you are enough to satisfy their hearts. Make them aware of even the slightest tendency to turn away from you to find happiness somewhere else. Cause them to see and understand how appalling and shocking it is for your children to turn away from you to find life. Help them to flee the futility of trying to find happiness through their own devices. Forgive them when they think about or pursue you in a casual way. Create in them a craving for you and your ways that surpasses every promise of pleasure in other things. Strengthen them to help those around them turn away from their futile ways and find fullness of joy in you. For your glory and their good, in Jesus' name, amen.

Write down any thoughts or ideas you may want to *Share*:

Notes

WEEK FIVE

Favor

To be grateful is to recognize the Love of God in everything He has given us—and He has given us everything. Every breath we draw is a gift of His Love, every moment of existence is a grace, for it brings with it immense graces from Him.
— DON POSTEMA

And whatever you do, in word or deed, do everything in the name of the Lord Jesus, giving thanks to God the Father through him. (Colossians 3:17)

...pray without ceasing, give thanks in all circumstances; for this is the will of God in Christ Jesus for you. (1 Thessalonians 5:17 18)

Day One of Favor

Father, open my eyes that I might *see* you more clearly, *savor* you more fully, and *share* you more freely.

Circle or underline any key words or phrases you *See*:

But by the grace of God I am what I am, and his grace toward me was not in vain. On the contrary, I worked harder than any of them, though it was not I, but the grace of God that is with me. (1 Corinthians 15:10)

Savor these truths in prayer:

Father, I pray that you would give _____ hearts that are tender and responsive to the grace and favor you have for them. Give them eyes to see glimpses of how powerful your grace is and how it gives them strength to pursue your purposes of steadfast love, justice, and righteousness in this world. Help them to believe that your grace is always at work behind the scenes to create goodness in their lives. Create in them a desire to be strengthened by your grace so that they may be a blessing to others. For your glory and their good, in the gracious name of Jesus, amen.

Write down any thoughts or ideas you may want to *Share*:

Day Two of Favor

Father, open my eyes that I might *see* you more clearly, *savor* you more fully, and *share* you more freely.

Circle or underline any key words or phrases you *See*:

Satisfy us in the morning with your steadfast love, that we may rejoice and be glad all our days. (Psalm 90:14)

Savor these truths in prayer:

Father, every day _____ will be presented with things that promise to make them happy and satisfy the longings of their hearts. I pray that you will help them see the greatness of your steadfast love as you display it in their lives, in your word, and in creation each day. Don't let them be tricked into believing that they would be more satisfied in life if they were smarter, stronger, prettier, or richer. You alone can satisfy their hearts and make them glad all their days. Awaken the taste buds of their hearts to enjoy the sweetness of your love every time they see it. Bring people into their lives that will help them delight in loving you. Help them learn to share their joy in your love more naturally and freely with others each day. For your glory and their good, in the all-satisfying name of Jesus, amen.

Write down any thoughts or ideas you may want to *Share*:

Day Three of Favor

Father, open my eyes that I might *see* you more clearly, *savor* you more fully, and *share* you more freely.

Circle or underline any key words or phrases you *See*:

"Glory to God in the highest, and on earth peace among those with whom he is pleased!" (Luke 2:14)

Now may the Lord of peace himself give you peace at all times in every way. The Lord be with you all. (2 Thessalonians 3:16)

Savor these truths in prayer:

Father, when your angels announced Jesus' arrival in the world, they declared glory to you and peace to us. Thank you that Jesus' coming declares your glory and our need. I pray for _____, that you would create in them a longing for the peace that you offer to the world through Jesus. Help them to identify any fears or anxieties that reside in their hearts about anything and bring it to you, that you would reign over it with your peace that surpasses all understanding. Help them to know that your peace in Jesus brings freedom that the world does not know. Cause them to become peacemakers to those around them. For your glory and their good, in the name of the Prince of Peace, Jesus, amen.

Write down any thoughts or ideas you may want to *Share*:

Day Four of Favor

Father, open my eyes that I might *see* you more clearly, *savor* you more fully, and *share* you more freely.

Circle or underline any key words or phrases you *See*:

What then shall we say to these things? If God is for us, who can be against us? He who did not spare his own Son but gave him up for us all, how will he not also with him graciously give us all things? (Romans 8:31-32)

Savor these truths in prayer:

Father, I pray today that _____ would sense the magnitude of your favor and goodness toward them. Let them be amazed by the fact that you are more than enough for whatever they face in this life. Let the truth that you are "for" them give them unbelievable courage to live for you in spite of their fears. Cause their confidence in you to be matched by a growing dependence on you, seeking your presence, protection, and provision each day. Show them that all the resources of heaven are theirs in Jesus. You have given the greatest gift of all in Jesus and I pray you would let the significance of his life, death, and resurrection sink into the depths of their hearts. Cause their trust in you to increase because of the truths of Romans 8:31-32. For your glory and their good, in Jesus' name, amen.

Write down any thoughts or ideas you may want to *Share*:

Day Five of Favor

Father, open my eyes that I might *see* you more clearly, *savor* you more fully, and *share* you more freely.

Circle or underline any key words or phrases you *See*:

Let the favor of the Lord our God be upon us, and establish the work of our hands upon us; yes, establish the work of our hands! (Psalm 90:17)

Savor these truths in prayer:

Father, I pray that _____ would know your favor in their work today, whether it is schoolwork or responsibilities around the home. Help them to realize that whatever they set their hands to do should be for your glory. You have created them for good works and they should devote themselves fully to the work to which you have called them. Establish the work of their hands, giving them a sense of accomplishment. Make it clear that your hand of favor is upon them through your provision, protection, presence, and purposes. Encourage them to find joy in their work, and make them a joy to work with. Cause them to study with diligence and delight in the truths they learn. For your glory and their good, in Jesus' name, amen.

Write down any thoughts or ideas you may want to *Share*:

Day Six of Favor

Father, open my eyes that I might *see* you more clearly, *savor* you more fully, and *share* you more freely.

Circle or underline any key words or phrases you *See*:

It is he who remembered us in our low estate, for his steadfast love endures forever; and rescued us from our foes, for his steadfast love endures forever; he who gives food to all flesh, for his steadfast love endures forever. Give thanks to the God of heaven, for his steadfast love endures forever. (Psalm 136:23-26)

Savor these truths in prayer:

Father, your steadfast love for _____ endures forever. It is through your grace and favor that they are able to know and experience your steadfast love toward them. If they are discouraged today, give them hope by reminding them that you love them. I pray that you would guard, protect, and rescue them from harm, and help them to have discernment in judging the intentions of others. Give them eyes to see the goodness of your provision every time they sit down to a meal. Stir up enduring thankfulness in them toward you and your favor. For your glory and their good, in the matchless name of Jesus, amen.

Write down any thoughts or ideas you may want to *Share*:

Day Seven of Favor

Father, open my eyes that I might *see* you more clearly, *savor* you more fully, and *share* you more freely.

Circle or underline any key words or phrases you *See*:

He [Jesus] is the image of the invisible God, the firstborn of all creation. For by him all things were created, in heaven and on earth, visible and invisible, whether thrones or dominions or rulers or authorities—all things were created through him and for him. And he is before all things, and in him all things hold together. (Colossians 1:15-17)

Savor these truths in prayer:

Father, thank you that you create and sustain all things. Your word declares that every day we are receiving your matchless favor through the sustaining power and goodness of Jesus. I pray that _____ would have a clear sense that they were not only created by Jesus, but also for Jesus. Fill their hearts and minds with delight in you that overflows in what they say and do. Let their lives give others hope in you as the creator and sustainer of life. Cause their delight in Jesus to continually increase, so that each day they would seek a deeper understanding of all that He is. For your glory and their good, in the matchless name of King Jesus, amen.

Write down any thoughts or ideas you may want to *Share*:

Notes

WEEK SIX

Wisdom

One of the beautiful aspects of prayer is that it is not just one directional. It is not just a cathartic experience where we unload on God to feel better. God communicates to us when we pray if we pause long enough to listen. God uses his Word and his Spirit to bring guidance, understanding, and conviction. You can be sure that he will never bring something to mind that is contrary to his Word. So ask him for guidance, understanding, and even conviction concerning anything in your world that needs to be addressed. Don't be afraid—he wants the best for you.

Search me, O God, and know my heart! Try me and know my thoughts! And see if there be any grievous way in me, and lead me in the way everlasting! (Psalm 139:23-24)

Day One of Wisdom

Father, open my eyes that I might *see* you more clearly, *savor* you more fully, and *share* you more freely.

Circle or underline any key words or phrases you *See*:

Thus says the LORD: "Let not the wise man boast in his wisdom, let not the mighty man boast in his might, let not the rich man boast in his riches, but let him who boasts boast in this, that he understands and knows me, that I am the LORD who practices steadfast love, justice, and righteousness in the earth. For in these things I delight, declares the LORD." (Jeremiah 9:23-24)

Savor these truths in prayer:

Father, I pray today that _____ would not boast or try to find their identity in how smart or insightful they are. Protect them from the lure of believing that their intelligence or insight makes them superior to other people. Cause their identity to be deeply rooted in you and their relationship with you, knowing that all of their abilities are gifts from you. Give them the wisdom that only comes from you to see where your love, justice, and righteousness are needed. Don't let them become cold or indifferent to the hardships around them. Give them a relentless resolve to apply your wisdom to these situations whole-heartedly, even when it is hard. Help me to encourage them and affirm all of the wisdom I see flowing from their lives. For your glory and their good, in Jesus' name, amen.

Write down any thoughts or ideas you may want to *Share*:

Day Two of Wisdom

Father, open my eyes that I might *see* you more clearly, *savor* you more fully, and *share* you more freely.

Circle or underline any key words or phrases you *See*:

Let no one deceive himself. If anyone among you thinks that he is wise in this age, let him become a fool that he may become wise. For the wisdom of this world is folly with God. For it is written, "He catches the wise in their craftiness," and again, "The Lord knows the thoughts of the wise, that they are futile." So let no one boast in men. For all things are yours, whether Paul or Apollos or Cephas or the world or life or death or the present or the future—all are yours, and you are Christ's, and Christ is God's. (1 Corinthians 3:18-23)

Savor these truths in prayer:

Father, it is so easy to be deceived into thinking that the ways of this world are wise. It is also easy to deceive ourselves into thinking we are wise on our own. I pray that you would protect _____ from traveling the path of self-proclaimed wisdom, which is the way of foolishness. Give them a keen sense of dependence on you so they can walk in humble confidence in you. Help them see the futility of trying to live by wisdom that is not rooted in you. Give them joy in turning to you in complete reliance, knowing that all things are yours and therefore their boast should be in you. Lastly, help me also to love and long for your wisdom above my own. For your glory and their good, in the supreme name of Christ, amen.

Write down any thoughts or ideas you may want to *Share*:

Day Three of Wisdom

Father, open my eyes that I might *see* you more clearly, *savor* you more fully, and *share* you more freely.

Circle or underline any key words or phrases you *See*:

I do not cease to give thanks for you, remembering you in my prayers, that the God of our Lord Jesus Christ, the Father of glory, may give you the Spirit of wisdom and of revelation in the knowledge of him, having the eyes of your hearts enlightened, that you may know what is the hope to which he has called you, what are the riches of his glorious inheritance in the saints, and what is the immeasurable greatness of his power toward us who believe, according to the working of his great might that he worked in Christ when he raised him from the dead... (Ephesians 1:16-20)

Savor these truths in prayer:

Father, I pray that you would give _____ your Spirit of wisdom, revelation, and knowledge. Enlighten the eyes of their hearts so that they might be eager to receive all the goodness that comes from each of these gifts. Even now as they are young, cause them to have an unwavering hope in the glorious inheritance you have prepared for them. Help them find rest and strength in your immeasurable power—the same power that raised Jesus from the dead. Empower them to live lives fueled by your Spirit. Make them like the apostle Paul who was a man of relentless thankfulness and purposeful prayer. For your glory and their good, in Jesus' name, amen.

Write down any thoughts or ideas you may want to *Share*:

Day Four of Wisdom

Father, open my eyes that I might *see* you more clearly, *savor* you more fully, and *share* you more freely.

Circle or underline any key words or phrases you *See*:

Walk in wisdom toward outsiders, making the best use of the time. (Colossians 4:5)

Look carefully then how you walk, not as unwise but as wise, making the best use of the time, because the days are evil. Therefore do not be foolish, but understand what the will of the Lord is. And do not get drunk with wine, for that is debauchery, but be filled with the Spirit... (Ephesians 5:15-18)

Savor these truths in prayer:

Father, I pray today for _____, that they would walk in wisdom in all of their relationships. Cause them to understand that their choices matter and to know that every decision leads to a destination. Give them incredible delight and persistence in turning away from evil and making the best use of their time. Even though they are young, give them a powerful desire to pursue your purposes with the time you have given them. Give them confidence that your will can be found in your Word. Your Word is the sword of the Spirit that is able to cut through the lies of this world. Give them a relentless desire to drink deeply of your Word every day so that they will be filled with your Spirit. For your glory and their good, in Jesus' name, amen.

Write down any thoughts or ideas you may want to *Share*:

Day Five of Wisdom

Father, open my eyes that I might *see* you more clearly, *savor* you more fully, and *share* you more freely.

Circle or underline any key words or phrases you *See*:

For I want you to know how great a struggle I have for you and for those at Laodicea and for all who have not seen me face to face, that their hearts may be encouraged, being knit together in love, to reach all the riches of full assurance of understanding and the knowledge of God's mystery, which is Christ, in whom are hidden all the treasures of wisdom and knowledge. I say this in order that no one may delude you with plausible arguments. (Colossians 2:2-4)

Savor these truths in prayer:

Father, I long for _____ to have hearts that are full of encouragement because they are unshakably bound in your love. Cause them to reach the fullness of knowing and understanding your mystery, which is Christ. Give them a deep understanding and joy, even as children, in all the treasures of wisdom and knowledge that are hidden in Christ. May they flourish in seeing, savoring and sharing the depths of wisdom and knowledge of Jesus with their peers. Let them be so captivated by the wonder of Jesus that they would never be duped to hope in something or someone else for life and joy. Use me to show them Jesus. For your glory and their good, in Jesus' name, amen.

Write down any thoughts or ideas you may want to *Share*:

Day Six of Wisdom

Father, open my eyes that I might *see* you more clearly, *savor* you more fully, and *share* you more freely.

Circle or underline any key words or phrases you *See*:

But as for you, continue in what you have learned and have firmly believed, knowing from whom you learned it and how from childhood you have been acquainted with the sacred writings, which are able to make you wise for salvation through faith in Christ Jesus. All Scripture is breathed out by God and profitable for teaching, for reproof, for correction, and for training in righteousness, that the man of God may be complete, equipped for every good work. (2 Timothy 3:14-17)

Savor these truths in prayer:

Father, there is nothing more important than knowing you personally and it is such a beautiful gift when that relationship begins early in life. Create in _____ tender hearts that are responsive to your Word so that they become wise for salvation through faith in Christ Jesus. Don't let them be deceived by the lies of this world; assure them that Jesus is the only way by which they can be saved and made right with you. Create in them teachable hearts and minds so that they may receive the full benefits of engaging with your Word. Bring people into their lives that help them grow to love your Word. Cause them to flourish in living out the truths of your Word. For your glory and their good, in Jesus' name, amen.

Write down any thoughts or ideas you may want to *Share*:

Day Seven of Wisdom

Father, open my eyes that I might *see* you more clearly, *savor* you more fully, and *share* you more freely.

Circle or underline any key words or phrases you *See*:

Who is wise and understanding among you? By his good conduct let him show his works in the meekness of wisdom . . . But the wisdom from above is first pure, then peaceable, gentle, open to reason, full of mercy and good fruits, impartial and sincere. And a harvest of righteousness is sown in peace by those who make peace. (James 3:13, 17-18)

Savor these truths in prayer:

Father, wise people bear fruit that reveals your wisdom. I pray that in these early years you would give _____ a hunger and thirst for your wisdom that is clearly a gift from you. Cause them to pursue it with diligent humility, leaving behind them a host of lives blessed by the fruit of the wisdom from above. Give them a keen ability to spot wisdom that is from you and embrace it as their own. Cause them to bear the fruit of wisdom that is pure, peaceful, gentle, open to reason, impartial, and sincere. Bring people into their lives who know and live out your wise purposes. May their lives produce a harvest of righteousness that is sown in peace. For your glory and their good, in the precious name of Jesus, amen.

Write down any thoughts or ideas you may want to *Share*:

Notes

WEEK SEVEN

Love

ive us, O Lord, a steadfast heart, which no unworthy affection may drag downwards; give us an unconquered heart, which no tribulation can wear out; give us an upright heart, which no unworthy purpose may tempt aside. Bestow upon us also, O Lord our God, understanding to know you, diligence to seek you, wisdom to find you, and a faithfulness that may finally embrace you; through Jesus Christ our Lord. — ST. THOMAS AQUINAS

Day One of Love

Father, open my eyes that I might *see* you more clearly, *savor* you more fully, and *share* you more freely.

Circle or underline any key words or phrases you *See*:

Love is patient and kind; love does not envy or boast; it is not arrogant or rude. It does not insist on its own way; it is not irritable or resentful; it does not rejoice at wrongdoing, but rejoices with the truth. Love bears all things, believes all things, hopes all things, endures all things. Love never ends. As for prophecies, they will pass away; as for tongues, they will cease; as for knowledge, it will pass away. (1 Corinthians 13:4-8)

Savor these truths in prayer:

Father, your love endures forever! I pray today that _____ would receive your love through other people. Grant that they would know your patience and feel your kindness throughout this day. Give them favor to encounter people filled with your love today. Cause them to become people who are marked by your love, showing patience and kindness especially when they encounter people who are arrogant and rude. May they be the sweet aroma of Christ to people who insist on their own way. Cause your supernatural love to empower them, even as children, to believe, hope, and endure all things. For your glory and their good, in Jesus' name, amen.

Write down any thoughts or ideas you may want to *Share*:

Day Two of Love

Father, open my eyes that I might *see* you more clearly, *savor* you more fully, and *share* you more freely.

Circle or underline any key words or phrases you *See*:

A new commandment I give to you, that you love one another: just as I have loved you, you also are to love one another. By this all people will know that you are my disciples, if you have love for one another. (John 13.34-35)

Savor these truths in prayer:

Father, I pray today for _____, that they would embrace your commandment to love one another. Give them eyes to see and hearts to understand how you have personally loved them. In your goodness provide them insight into just how deep, wide, long, and high your love is for them. Create in them a strong desire and will to show love to others. May their obedience to your command to love one another cause the people in their worlds to know that they are your disciples. Protect them from becoming casual or indifferent in how they care for those around them. Help them experience your love deeply so they can love others deeply. Show me how you can use me as an agent of your love. For your glory and their good, in Jesus' name, amen.

Write down any thoughts or ideas you may want to *Share*:

Day Three of Love

Father, open my eyes that I might *see* you more clearly, *savor* you more fully, and *share* you more freely.

Circle or underline any key words or phrases you *See*:

There is no fear in love, but perfect love casts out fear. For fear has to do with punishment, and whoever fears has not been perfected in love. We love because he first loved us. If anyone says, "I love God," and hates his brother, he is a liar; for he who does not love his brother whom he has seen cannot love God whom he has not seen. And this commandment we have for him: whoever loves God must also love his brother. (1 John 4:18-21)

Savor these truths in prayer:

Father, give _____ eyes to see their fears and help them to have complete confidence that your perfect love can neutralize those fears. Cause them to run to you with each and every fear so that they may be swallowed up by your perfect love. There is a profound freedom that comes from knowing your deep and abiding love. Help their young hearts soak in your fear-killing and freedom-producing love like a brand new sponge. Where their love is weak, strengthen it. Make their hearts grow large in love towards you and man. Help them to learn to love others in the same way they have received love from you. For your glory and their good, in the loving name of Jesus, amen.

Write down any thoughts or ideas you may want to *Share*:

Day Four of Love

Father, open my eyes that I might *see* you more clearly, *savor* you more fully, and *share* you more freely.

Circle or underline any key words or phrases you *See:*

In this the love of God was made manifest among us, that God sent his only Son into the world, so that we might live through him. In this is love, not that we have loved God but that he loved us and sent his Son to be the propitiation for our sins. Beloved, if God so loved us, we also ought to love one another. (1 John 4:9-11)

Savor these truths in prayer:

Father, thank you for making your love clear in Jesus! I pray that you would give _____ an ever-deepening sense of the importance of your love for them in sending your Son into the world. Help them see that their sins have separated them from you, and you solved that separation through Jesus' sacrifice. Let them understand your amazing goodness in sending Jesus to take the full amount of your wrath for their sins. Cause their hearts to be filled with overflowing thankfulness for your sacrificial love. May that love be one of the distinguishing marks of their lives. Help them love one another the way that you have loved them in Jesus. Give them eyes to see how they can show your love to others today. For your glory and their good, in Jesus' name, amen.

Write down any thoughts or ideas you may want to *Share:*

Day Five of Love

Father, open my eyes that I might *see* you more clearly, *savor* you more fully, and *share* you more freely.

Circle or underline any key words or phrases you *See*:

For God so loved the world, that he gave his only Son, that whoever believes in him should not perish but have eternal life. For God did not send his Son into the world to condemn the world, but in order that the world might be saved through him. Whoever believes in him is not condemned, but whoever does not believe is condemned already, because he has not believed in the name of the only Son of God. (John 3:16-18)

Savor these truths in prayer:

Father, I pray that in your grace you would be generous in giving _____ eyes to see the scope of your love for the world. The world is big and yet your love is even bigger. Create in them a desire to grow in their understanding of the depth of your personal sacrifice by sending your Son, Jesus to pay the penalty of their sins. Increase their confidence that Jesus is the only way of entering eternal life. Help them learn to embrace the weight of the truth that not believing in Jesus, the only Son of God, results in condemnation. Give them a relentless desire to invite unbelievers to put their trust in Jesus alone for life, a life that starts now and lasts forever. For your glory and their good, in the saving name of Jesus, amen.

Write down any thoughts or ideas you may want to *Share*:

Day Six of Love

Father, open my eyes that I might *see* you more clearly, *savor* you more fully, and *share* you more freely.

Circle or underline any key words or phrases you *See*:

Beloved, let us love one another, for love is from God, and whoever loves has been born of God and knows God. Anyone who does not love does not know God, because God is love. (1 John 4:7 8)

Savor these truths in prayer:

Father, I pray for _____, that you would open their eyes to see that you are the source of all love, because you are love. I pray that you would be lavish in pouring your love into their lives. Grant that they would grow in their understanding of what it means to know you and to be born of you. Cause them to love others deeply out of their own growing relationship with you. Keep them from ever minimizing the importance of loving others well. Help them to be aware of any tendency to shrug it off or take it lightly when they hold onto a grudge, are bitter, or disrespectful of others. Help them to embrace the truth that without a life marked by love, we cannot really know you because you are love! For your glory and their good, in Jesus' name, amen.

Write down any thoughts or ideas you may want to *Share*:

Day Seven of Love

Father, open my eyes that I might *see* you more clearly, *savor* you more fully, and *share* you more freely.

Circle or underline any key words or phrases you *See*:

"But I say to you who hear, Love your enemies, do good to those who hate you, bless those who curse you, pray for those who abuse you... "If you love those who love you, what benefit is that to you? For even sinners love those who love them... Be merciful, even as your Father is merciful. (Luke 6:27, 28, 33, 36)

Savor these truths in prayer:

Father, thank you that your love is unlike anything the world has ever known. I pray that _____ would taste and see that you are good and that your love has power to transform relationships. Help them to embrace your desire for them to love their enemies by doing them good and praying for them. Help them to see when their response to their enemies looks more like the world's than yours. In your mercy, I pray that you would give them hearts that are filled with mercy toward others. Cause them to see that how they treat others, especially their adversaries, is really important. May you receive great glory from their obedience in loving the most difficult to love. For your glory and their good, in the all-powerful name of Jesus Christ, amen.

Write down any thoughts or ideas you may want to *Share*:

Notes

Faith

Praying for your child by yourself is valuable, but I want to encourage you to consider widening your circle. Find a friend who is also a Prayer Champion and pray together perhaps once a week. If that's too big a commitment for you, consider doing it once a month. You will find that praying this prayer guide with someone is easy and incredibly encouraging. You may find it so encouraging that you create a Prayer Champions' prayer group to strengthen your efforts of interceding for the next generation!

For where two or three are gathered in my name, there am I among them. (Matthew 18:20)

Day One of Faith

Father, open my eyes that I might *see* you more clearly, *savor* you more fully, and *share* you more freely.

Circle or underline any key words or phrases you *See*:

And without faith it is impossible to please him, for whoever would draw near to God must believe that he exists and that he rewards those who seek him (Hebrews 11:6)

Savor these truths in prayer:

Father, I pray for _____ today, that you would capture their hearts and minds with the truths of this passage. Instill in their hearts a relentless desire to please you even now while they are young. Protect them from the cultural disease of indifference or apathy concerning what pleases you. Help them to understand that without faith it is impossible to please you. Cause them to learn to take you at your Word and to use the Scriptures to fuel their faith to trust you with every struggle they encounter. Give them faith to believe that you are alive and ready to work on their behalf when they seek you with their whole heart. Be the object of their faith and may their reward be a heart that is satisfied with all that you are for them. For your glory and their good, in Jesus' name, amen.

Write down any thoughts or ideas you may want to *Share*:

Day Two of Faith

Father, open my eyes that I might *see* you more clearly, *savor* you more fully, and *share* you more freely.

Circle or underline any key words or phrases you *See*:

Therefore, since we are surrounded by so great a cloud of witnesses, let us also lay aside every weight, and sin which clings so closely, and let us run with endurance the race that is set before us, looking to Jesus, the founder and perfecter of our faith, who for the joy that was set before him endured the cross, despising the shame, and is seated at the right hand of the throne of God. (Hebrews 12:1-2)

Savor these truths in prayer:

Father, thank you that as your children you have called _____ to run the race of faith that is set before them. Inspire them to run strong as they learn about all the saints that have gone before them. Give them endurance to be finishers of the race and not just beginners. Help them learn that the race of faith is a marathon and not a sprint. Teach them to be quick to let go of every kind of sin that would hold them back from running freely. Give them the focus to set their sights on you, Jesus, as the author and perfecter of their faith. Give them joy in you that captures their hearts and propels them forward in faith to do great things for your glory. May you be praised forever! In Jesus' name, amen.

Write down any thoughts or ideas you may want to *Share*:

Day Three of Faith

Father, open my eyes that I might *see* you more clearly, *savor* you more fully, and *share* you more freely.

Circle or underline any key words or phrases you *See:*

You keep him in perfect peace whose mind is stayed on you, because he trusts in you. Trust in the LORD forever, for the LORD GOD is an everlasting rock. (Isaiah 26.3-4)

Savor these truths in prayer:

Father, your presence is a place of perfect peace where you keep those whose minds are focused on you. I pray that _____ would learn to fix their minds on you today with absolute trust. Give them a strong growing confidence in you that endures throughout their entire lives. Establish them in your perfect peace, knowing that you are their God and their everlasting rock. Give them the ability to see fear, worry, and anxiety as signals to turn to you in faith so that your perfect peace would reign in their hearts. Let their peace and faith in you free them to have the courage to risk loving and caring for the people that you bring into their lives. Cause them to know that you are the only trustworthy source in which they can place their faith. For your glory and their good, in Jesus' name, amen.

Write down any thoughts or ideas you may want to *Share:*

Day Four of Faith

Father, open my eyes that I might *see* you more clearly, *savor* you more fully, and *share* you more freely.

Circle or underline any key words or phrases you *See*:

And Jesus said to him, "If you can! All things are possible for one who believes." Immediately the father of the child cried out and said, "I believe; help my unbelief!" (Mark 9:23-24)

Savor these truths in prayer:

Father, thank you for the powerful promises you give us in your Word. Thank you for the hope that you offer to your children who trust you with their lives. I pray that you would give _____ the ability to see and feel their own personal neediness for you in their lives. Give them eyes to see the beauty of your promises for their lives. Help them to know that feeling helpless can be one of your greatest gifts to them when they respond by calling out to you in humility for help. Teach them to know that all things are possible with you. Give them a daily desire to call out to you for more faith, "I believe! Help my unbelief!" Give them pleasure in trusting you in prayer. Use me to encourage them in pursuing you! For your glory and their good, in the faithful name of Jesus, amen.

Write down any thoughts or ideas you may want to *Share*:

Day Five of Faith

Father, open my eyes that I might *see* you more clearly, *savor* you more fully, and *share* you more freely.

Circle or underline any key words or phrases you *See*:

To this end we always pray for you, that our God may make you worthy of his calling and may fulfill every resolve for good and every work of faith by his power, so that the name of our Lord Jesus may be glorified in you, and you in him, according to the grace of our God and the Lord Jesus Christ. (2 Thessalonians 1:11-12)

Savor these truths in prayer:

Father, I pray for _____ today, that you would show them your goodness in giving them a calling on their lives. Help them to know that even as children, you are working in and through them to accomplish the things they are willing to trust you for. Teach them that every act of faith brings glory to your name because of your empowering grace. Help them to find great joy in knowing that you are always with them, making them worthy of your calling on their lives. May the world know that they are your precious and loved children as they trust you each day. For your glory and their good, in Jesus' name, amen.

Write down any thoughts or ideas you may want to *Share*:

Day Six of Faith

Father, open my eyes that I might *see* you more clearly, *savor* you more fully, and *share* you more freely.

Circle or underline any key words or phrases you *See*:

Fight the good fight of the faith. Take hold of the eternal life to which you were called and about which you made the good confession in the presence of many witnesses. (1 Timothy 6:12)

I have fought the good fight, I have finished the race, I have kept the faith. Henceforth there is laid up for me the crown of righteousness... (2 Timothy 4:7-8)

Savor these truths in prayer:

Father, I pray that _____ would learn that being your follower is a fight of faith to believe your good and perfect promises over the deceptive promises of the world, the flesh, and the devil. Help them understand that eternal life is real. Give them a growing sense that being with you for all eternity is of utmost importance. Instill in them as children a desire to fight the good fight of faith with focus and persistence. Give them childlike faith to yield their hearts to you and the power of your Spirit to believe all that you have promised. Give them delight in the truth that you have prepared a place for them as their Savior, Redeemer, and King. May the promise of eternal life with you compel them to fight the good fight of faith. For your glory and their good. In Jesus' name, amen.

Write down any thoughts or ideas you may want to *Share*:

Day Seven of Faith

Father, open my eyes that I might *see* you more clearly, *savor* you more fully, and *share* you more freely.

Circle or underline any key words or phrases you *See*:

…and I pray that the sharing of your faith may become effective for the full knowledge of every good thing that is in us for the sake of Christ. (Philemon 1:6)

Savor these truths in prayer:

Father, I pray that _____ would fall more and more deeply in love with you. Cause their love for you to be strong so that they would freely and naturally share their faith with others. Give them joy in seeing others come to trust you alone with their salvation and every aspect of their lives. Cause them to understand that sharing their faith actually deepens their faith in you and all of your promises for them. As they share their faith, give them eyes to see your glory, steadfast love, and faithfulness all along the way. Establish in their hearts the full knowledge of every good thing that is theirs because of Christ. Give them your favor as they speak on your behalf in this world. Soften the hearts of those who hear of your goodness through them. For your glory and their good, in Jesus' name, amen.

Write down any thoughts or ideas you may want to *Share*:

Notes

WEEK NINE

Purity

If we don't feel strong desires for the manifestation of the glory of God, it is not because we have drunk deeply and are satisfied. It is because we have nibbled so long at the table of the world. Our soul is stuffed with small things, and there is no room for the great.
—JOHN PIPER

Day One of Purity

Father, open my eyes that I might *see* you more clearly, *savor* you more fully, and *share* you more freely.

Circle or underline any key words or phrases you *See*:

No temptation has overtaken you that is not common to man. God is faithful, and he will not let you be tempted beyond your ability, but with the temptation he will also provide the way of escape, that you may be able to endure it. (1 Corinthians 10:13)

Savor these truths in prayer:

Father, thank you for the reminder that the temptations that we face are common to all mankind. The enemy of our souls wants us to believe that we are alone in our sin and temptations, but you have assured us that this is not the case. I pray that _____ would know that their temptations are not unique to them. Help them to know that you will help them overcome their temptations. Give them faith to believe your promise that you will not allow them to be tempted beyond their ability. Don't let them forget that your promise of success is accompanied by a call to endure. Forge in them a faith that depends completely on the power of your Spirit. For your glory and their good, in Jesus' name, amen.

Write down any thoughts or ideas you may want to *Share*:

Day Two of Purity

Father, open my eyes that I might *see* you more clearly, *savor* you more fully, and *share* you more freely.

Circle or underline any key words or phrases you *See*:

For this is the will of God, your sanctification: that you abstain from sexual immorality; that each one of you know how to control his body in holiness and honor, not in the passion of lust like the Gentiles who do not know God...For God has not called us for impurity, but in holiness. Therefore whoever disregards this, disregards not man but God, who gives his Holy Spirit to you. (1 Thessalonians 4:3-5, 7-8)

Savor these truths in prayer:

Father, thank you for making your will for our lives known. It is your will that we be sanctified or made holy specifically in our sexual relationships. I pray that you would er _____ to abstain from all sexual immorality. Protect them in their personal relationships and guard their eyes against anything that would promote or demonstrate immoral relationships. Protect them from the devastating lure of lust. Give them discernment and desire for purity, and create seriousness in their hearts concerning how they control their bodies. Father, our holiness is serious to you because you are holy. Help us to embrace the truth that to disregard your calling on our lives for purity is to disregard you. For your glory and their good, in Jesus' name, amen.

Write down any thoughts or ideas you may want to *Share*:

Day Three of Purity

Father, open my eyes that I might *see* you more clearly, *savor* you more fully, and *share* you more freely.

Circle or underline any key words or phrases you **See**:

Do not love the world or the things in the world. If anyone loves the world, the love of the Father is not in him. For all that is in the world—the desires of the flesh and the desires of the eyes and pride of life—is not from the Father but is from the world. And the world is passing away along with its desires, but whoever does the will of God abides forever. (1 John 2:15-17)

Savor these truths in prayer:

Father, you are clear in what is good for us and what is not. Too often our appetites lead us astray. Father, I pray that you would give _____ an appetite that causes supreme delight and enjoyment in you. Keep earthly loves from creeping into their hearts. Grant them an acute awareness of when they are being lured into the desires of the flesh. Give them eyes to see the futility in loving the things of this world. Cause their love for you to increase and abound in depth, breadth, length, and height. For your glory and their good. In Jesus' name, amen.

Write down any thoughts or ideas you may want to **Share**:

Day Four of Purity

Father, open my eyes that I might *see* you more clearly, *savor* you more fully, and *share* you more freely.

Circle or underline any key words or phrases you *See*:

Now to him who is able to keep you from stumbling and to present you blameless before the presence of his glory with great joy, to the only God, our Savior, through Jesus Christ our Lord, be glory, majesty, dominion, and authority, before all time and now and forever. Amen. (Jude 1:24-25)

Savor these truths in prayer:

Father, I commit _____ to you today. You alone are able to keep them from stumbling and make them blameless in your presence. Don't let them get sidetracked by sin and temptation. Capture their minds and hearts with the wonder of one day entering into the presence of your glory. Cause them to move steadily toward you and your purposes. Make them long for you and your presence. May your name be blessed and praised forever. In Jesus' name, amen.

Write down any thoughts or ideas you may want to *Share*:

Day Five of Purity

Father, open my eyes that I might *see* you more clearly, *savor* you more fully, and *share* you more freely.

Circle or underline any key words or phrases you *See*:

Create in me a clean heart, O God, and renew a right spirit within me. Cast me not away from your presence, and take not your Holy Spirit from me. Restore to me the joy of your salvation, and uphold me with a willing spirit. (Psalm 51:10-12)

Savor these truths in prayer:

Father, only you can create a clean heart and renew a right spirit within us. Cause _____ to be discontented until they have come to you, so that you can cleanse their hearts and renew a right spirit within them. Help them to feel the weight of their disobedience toward you. Please do not let them become comfortable with unconfessed sin in their lives. Give them a longing to be in your presence. Help them to know the Holy Spirit's leading and conviction. Grant that they would desire more than anything the restoration of the joy of your salvation. May they rejoice in the sustaining power of your Spirit. For your glory and their good, in Jesus' name, amen.

Write down any thoughts or ideas you may want to *Share*:

Day Six of Purity

Father, open my eyes that I might *see* you more clearly, *savor* you more fully, and *share* you more freely.

Circle or underline any key words or phrases you *See*:

Now may the God of peace himself sanctify you completely, and may your whole spirit and soul and body be kept blameless at the coming of our Lord Jesus Christ. He who calls you is faithful, he will surely do it. Brothers, pray for us. (1 Thessalonians 5:23-25)

Savor these truths in prayer:

Father, I praise you as the God of Peace. I call upon you to sanctify _____ completely. Please keep their whole spirit and body blameless before you. I stand in awe of your perfect faithfulness to your children. Thank you that you finish your work in each one of them. Don't let them wander from the truth, and help them yield to your will daily. May you enable them to embrace the sanctification process, letting go of sin and the weights that hold them back. Cause them to move forward, filled with your powerful peace. For your glory and their good, in Jesus' name, amen.

Write down any thoughts or ideas you may want to *Share*:

Day Seven of Purity

Father, open my eyes that I might *see* you more clearly, *savor* you more fully, and *share* you more freely.

Circle or underline any key words or phrases you *See*:

Every way of a man is right in his own eyes, but the LORD weighs the heart. (Proverbs 21:2)

All the ways of a man are pure in his own eyes, but the LORD weighs the spirit. (Proverbs 16:2)

The heart is deceitful above all things, and desperately sick; who can understand it? "I the LORD search the heart and test the mind..." (Jeremiah 17:9-10)

Savor these truths in prayer:

Father, ever since we turned from you in the garden, we have thought that our way was the best way. Your way is always best. Forgive us for being deceived in thinking that our way is ever the right way. I pray today that _____ would know the truth about their hearts. Cause them to walk humbly with you, the one who knows and understands their inmost thoughts and intentions. Transform their hearts to be in tune with you and your purposes, making them tender and teachable towards you and others. Cause them to submit to your Spirit and your Word, guiding and directing them in the way they should go. For your glory and their good, in Jesus' name, amen.

Write down any thoughts or ideas you may want to *Share*:

Notes

WEEK TEN

Speech

One of the designs of this book is to help you make praying the Scriptures for the next generation as natural as breathing. Unlike breathing, though, identifying key passages and turning them into prayers takes a little practice. In Week Thirteen you will have the opportunity to create your own prayers. So with that in mind, I encourage you to start taking note of any words or phrases that are especially encouraging or inspiring as you are praying. Also, be on the hunt for portions of Scripture that you would like to make the focus of your prayers. Remember to ask God for his favor while you create prayers that will bless your child.

Day One of Speech

Father, open my eyes that I might *see* you more clearly, *savor* you more fully, and *share* you more freely.

Circle or underline any key words or phrases you *See*:

Let no corrupting talk come out of your mouths, but only such as is good for building up, as fits the occasion, that it may give grace to those who hear. (Ephesians 4:29)

Let there be no filthiness nor foolish talk nor crude joking, which are out of place, but instead let there be thanksgiving. (Ephesians 5:4)

Savor these truths in prayer:

Father, we live in a world that is so often careless and crude in how we use our speech. I pray that you would protect _____ from speech that can corrupt and tear them down. Help them to see destructive speech and never become comfortable with it from their friends or from themselves. Give them a strong desire and determination to only use words that encourage others. Help them to learn to speak good words with purpose and precision. Guard them from speech that is filled with filthiness and crude joking. Help them to learn to initiate conversations that are gracious, encouraging, and filled with gratefulness for all that you have done for them. Make thankfulness their primary way they battle speech around them that is filled with foolishness, or crude joking, so that you are glorified and others are uplifted. For your glory and their good, in Jesus' name, amen.

Write down any thoughts or ideas you may want to *Share*:

Day Two of Speech

Father, open my eyes that I might *see* you more clearly, *savor* you more fully, and *share* you more freely.

Circle or underline any key words or phrases you *See*:

...do not be anxious about anything, but in everything by prayer and supplication with thanksgiving let your requests be made known to God. And the peace of God, which surpasses all understanding, will guard your hearts and your minds in Christ Jesus. (Philippians 4:6-7)

Savor these truths in prayer:

Father, there is so much in life that is out of our control which can lead to fear and anxiety. Thank you that you are sufficient for all things in our lives and that there is nothing outside of your control. I pray that _____ would learn to place their hope and trust in you in all circumstances. Cause their natural response to uncertainty be prayer that is filled with thanksgiving to Jesus as the one who holds all things together by the power of his Word. Make your promise of peace surpass all their understanding when they pray, flooding their hearts and minds in Christ. Make fear or anxiety flee their hearts and minds, as they trust you in prayer. Help them learn to offer prayers that are saturated with thanksgiving for all that you are. Cause them to learn to pray without ceasing, making it their most-used form of speech. For your glory and their good, in Jesus' name, amen.

Write down any thoughts or ideas you may want to *Share*:

Day Three of Speech

Father, open my eyes that I might *see* you more clearly, *savor* you more fully, and *share* you more freely.

Circle or underline any key words or phrases you *See*:

Continue steadfastly in prayer, being watchful in it with thanksgiving. At the same time, pray also for us, that God may open to us a door for the word, to declare the mystery of Christ, on account of which I am in prison—that I may make it clear, which is how I ought to speak. (Colossians 4:2-4)

Savor these truths in prayer:

Father, thank you for the gift of being able to talk to you in prayer. It is my hope and prayer for _____ today that speaking to you in prayer would become as natural as breathing. Just as breathing sustains their physical lives, help them understand that steadfastness in prayer sustains their relationship with you. Help them to learn to be alert to the needs for prayer around them. Give them so much confidence and hope in you that all of their prayers would have a flavor of worship and thankfulness. I pray specifically that you would grow their desire to see the mystery of Christ proclaimed. Give them the willingness and ability to share the wonders of what you have done in Christ freely and frequently. Grant that they would not only share your greatness clearly and simply but that they would help others find freedom in sharing you as well. For your glory and their good, in Jesus' name, amen.

Write down any thoughts or ideas you may want to *Share*:

Day Four of Speech

Father, open my eyes that I might *see* you more clearly, *savor* you more fully, and *share* you more freely.

Circle or underline any key words or phrases you *See*:

Let your speech always be gracious, seasoned with salt, so that you may know how you ought to answer each person. (Colossians 4:6)

Savor these truths in prayer:

Father, I pray today that you would bless _____ with your favor and wisdom especially in how they talk with others. Give them gracious speech. Teach them that gracious speech is humble speech and is not boastful or proud. Help them learn to help others flourish in life with the words they speak. Create in them speech that is gracious and seasoned with your wisdom so that they will know how to answer everyone who engages with them. Cause them even as children to become magnets for good conversations that build others up and that honor you. Give them friends who also desire to speak words that are gracious and encouraging. May the words they speak be used to create a hunger and thirst for you and your truth. For your glory and their good, in Jesus' name, amen.

Write down any thoughts or ideas you may want to *Share*:

Day Five of Speech

Father, open my eyes that I might *see* you more clearly, *savor* you more fully, and *share* you more freely.

Circle or underline any key words or phrases you *See*:

Have nothing to do with foolish, ignorant controversies; you know that they breed quarrels. And the Lord's servant must not be quarrelsome but kind to everyone, able to teach, patiently enduring evil, correcting his opponents with gentleness. God may perhaps grant them repentance leading to a knowledge of the truth... (2 Timothy 2:23-25)

Savor these truths in prayer:

Father, I pray that you would protect _____ today from foolish speech. It is so easy to be proud and engage in arguments that do not even matter. Give them wisdom to know when a pointless argument is starting up in conversation and help them learn to become a peacemaker when quarrels erupt. Even as children I pray that you would fill them with your kindness and patience in all their conversations. Give them the ability to teach others about you in a gentle and loving way so that perhaps they might turn to you in faith believing the truth. Give them a desire to please you with how they speak with others. May you be praised for all the gracious ways your children speak. In Jesus' name, amen.

Write down any thoughts or ideas you may want to *Share*:

Day Six of Speech

Father, open my eyes that I might *see* you more clearly, *savor* you more fully, and *share* you more freely.

Circle or underline any key words or phrases you *See*:

Rejoice always, pray without ceasing, give thanks in all circumstances; for this is the will of God in Christ Jesus for you. (1 Thessalonians 5:16-18)
   We give thanks to God always for all of you, constantly mentioning you in our prayers... (1 Thessalonians 1:2)

Savor these truths in prayer:

Father, thank you for clearly revealing your will for us in Christ Jesus. I pray that _____ would have a lifestyle that is marked by rejoicing, prayer, and thankfulness. Cause them to find joy in your goodness each day, and help them to express that joy through praise to you. Create in them a longing to see your greatness each day, and help them express their longing in relentless prayer. Help their prayers to be saturated with thankfulness for all things in all circumstances. Give them eyes to see the good you are doing in and through others. Cause their hearts to overflow in thankfulness toward you. For your glory and their good, in Jesus' name, amen.

Write down any thoughts or ideas you may want to *Share*:

Day Seven of Speech

Father, open my eyes that I might *see* you more clearly, *savor* you more fully, and *share* you more freely.

Circle or underline any key words or phrases you *See*:

Therefore God has highly exalted him and bestowed on him the name that is above every name, so that at the name of Jesus every knee should bow, in heaven and on earth and under the earth, and every tongue confess that Jesus Christ is Lord, to the glory of God the Father. (Philippians 2:9-11)

...for it is written, "As I live, says the Lord, every knee shall bow to me, and every tongue confess to God." (Romans 14:11)

Savor these truths in prayer:

Father, thank you that Jesus is Lord over all things and that you are highly exalted above all other competitors for your glory whether in heaven or earth. I pray that you would help _____ see and savor your Lordship for all it is worth. Cause their hearts to grow in love and adoration for you as they learn more about your greatness. Help them understand that one day every knee everywhere will bow before your greatness. Give them understanding that every person on this planet will one day confess that Jesus is Lord and that confession will bring massive glory to you. Give them joy in telling their peers how great you are even now as they look to the day when everyone will sing your praises. For your glory and their good, in Jesus' name, amen.

Write down any thoughts or ideas you may want to *Share*:

Notes

WEEK ELEVEN

Conduct

P rayer is asking God to incarnate, to get dirty in your life. Yes, the
eternal God scrubs floors. For sure we know he washes feet. So take
Jesus at his word. Ask him. Tell him what you want. Get dirty. Write
out your prayer requests; don't mindlessly drift through life on the
American narcotic of busyness. If you try to seize the day, the day will
eventually break you. Seize the corner of his garment and don't let go
until he blesses you. He will reshape the day. — PAUL E. MILLER

Humble yourselves, therefore, under the mighty hand of God so that
at the proper time he may exalt you, casting all your anxieties on him,
because he cares for you. (1 Peter 5:6-7)

Day One of Conduct

Father, open my eyes that I might *see* you more clearly, *savor* you more fully, and *share* you more freely.

Circle or underline any key words or phrases you *See*:

I am the vine; you are the branches. Whoever abides in me and I in him, he it is that bears much fruit, for apart from me you can do nothing. (John 15:5)

Savor these truths in prayer:

Father, thank you that you are our great and glorious creator and sustainer. I pray that you would cause _____ to have a growing sense that their lives are yours and that they are dependent on you for everything. Give them eyes to see, ears to hear, and hearts that understand how your sustaining provision causes them to flourish when they hope and trust in you. Give them a desire to flourish in the way they live and thus a strong desire to abide in and rest in you. Help them to know that apart from you they can do nothing. Don't let them be deceived into thinking that they can pull themselves up by their own bootstraps. Give them a clear understanding that you are the one who gives them the strength to even put on their boots. Empower them by your Spirit to bear fruit that lasts. Give them a longing to abide in you and help others to come and find their greatest satisfaction in you. For your glory and their good, in Jesus' name, amen.

Write down any thoughts or ideas you may want to *Share*:

Day Two of Conduct

Father, open my eyes that I might *see* you more clearly, *savor* you more fully, and *share* you more freely.

Circle or underline any key words or phrases you *See*:

Therefore, since we have been justified by faith, we have peace with God through our Lord Jesus Christ. Through him we have also obtained access by faith into this grace in which we stand, and we rejoice in hope of the glory of God. Not only that, but rejoice in our sufferings, knowing that suffering produces endurance, and endurance produces character, and character produces hope, and hope does not put us to shame, because God's love has been poured into our hearts through the Holy Spirit who has been given to us. (Romans 5:1-5)

Savor these truths in prayer:

Father, I praise you for your great work in _____ today. Bless them today with a growing understanding of the wonder of your grace that makes it possible for them to know you through Jesus. Give them grace to know that every trial they face has a purpose that is often bigger than what they can see. By your mercy help them to see glimpses of the character and hope you are forging in their lives. Cause them to see and savor the lavish love you have poured into their hearts by the Holy Spirit. Fill their hearts and mouths with praise for all of the goodness that results from enduring through hardships. May their hope in you always propel them forward in faith. For your glory and their good, in Jesus' name, amen.

Write down any thoughts or ideas you may want to *Share*:

Day Three of Conduct

Father, open my eyes that I might *see* you more clearly, *savor* you more fully, and *share* you more freely.

Circle or underline any key words or phrases you *See*:

His master said to him, 'Well done, good and faithful servant. You have been faithful over a little; I will set you over much. Enter into the joy of your master.' (Matthew 25:21)

For we are his workmanship, created in Christ Jesus for good works which God prepared beforehand, that we should walk in them. (Ephesians 2:10)

Savor these truths in prayer:

Father, thank you that you have created _____ for your glory. Thank you for the natural abilities and specific personalities you have given them to accomplish your purposes. I pray that they would long to fulfill the purposes and please you even as children. Give them a tenacity of purpose and joy that is fueled by your love for them. Cause them to live faithfully for you even when it is hard, knowing that they are your workmanship, created in Christ Jesus to make a lasting difference in this world. Help them to start their journey of faith with you well, but more importantly I pray that you would empower them to finish well. Give them strength to persevere so that they hear your marvelous words: "Well done, good and faithful servant" and "Enter into the joy of your master." For your glory and their good, in Jesus' name, amen.

Write down any thoughts or ideas you may want to *Share*:

Day Four of Conduct

Father, open my eyes that I might *see* you more clearly, *savor* you more fully, and *share* you more freely.

Circle or underline any key words or phrases you *See*:

You are the light of the world. A city set on a hill cannot be hidden. Nor do people light a lamp and put it under a basket, but on a stand, and it gives light to all in the house. In the same way, let your light shine before others, so that they may see your good works and give glory to your Father who is in heaven. (Matthew 5:14-16)

Savor these truths in prayer:

Father, you have called us to shine in such a way that the world will know you are great. I pray that _____ would grow in their understanding that their life purpose is to show how great you are. Protect them from a spirit of fear that would cause them to hide their light behind shyness or fear. Create in them courage to do works of love, kindness, mercy, and justice so that the world might be drawn to the beauty of Jesus. Give them as sense of risk for the glory of God. Give them a clear sense of the presence of the Holy Spirit working in them to make Jesus known to the world. Bless them with understanding of how to serve you and others that would help them to trust you with their lives. Give them freedom in helping others find the joy of serving and glorifying you through their good works. May you be praised forever, in Jesus' name, amen.

Write down any thoughts or ideas you may want to *Share*:

Day Five of Conduct

Father, open my eyes that I might *see* you more clearly, *savor* you more fully, and *share* you more freely.

Circle or underline any key words or phrases you *See*:

Live in harmony with one another. Do not be haughty, but associate with the lowly. Never be wise in your own sight. Repay no one evil for evil, but give thought to do what is honorable in the sight of all. If possible, so far as it depends on you, live peaceably with all. (Romans 12:16-18)

Savor these truths in prayer:

Father, you are worthy of all praise and sacrifice. All of your commands are designed for our good. Thank you for the admonitions in this passage that show us how to live a life that flourishes with others. I pray that _____ would find joy in pursuing a life of harmony with others. Protect them from ever thinking that they are better than others. Give them eyes to see when they are beginning to become haughty and proud. Cause them to feel freedom in engaging with those who are less fortunate, knowing that everything they have is by your gracious hand. Create in them the character of Christ that is full of forgiveness. Give them the power of your spirit to do what is honorable in the sight of all, just as Jesus did when he unjustly suffered. Create in them a passionate desire to live at peace with everyone. For your glory and their good, in Jesus' name, amen.

Write down any thoughts or ideas you may want to *Share*:

Day Six of Conduct

Father, open my eyes that I might *see* you more clearly, *savor* you more fully, and *share* you more freely.

Circle or underline any key words or phrases you *See*:

So whether you eat or drink, or whatever you do, do all to the glory of God.
(1 Corinthians 10:31)

And whatever you do, in word or deed, do everything in the name of the
Lord Jesus, giving thanks to God the Father through him. (Colossians 3:17)

Savor these truths in prayer:

Father, thank you that _____'s lives belong to you. You created them by your power and for your glory. It is only when they live for your glory that their lives can be fulfilled. I pray that you would draw them to yourself today so they would know the sweetness and power of your presence. Even as children I ask that you would give them strength, desire, and passion to do everything they do today for your glory. Help them to give thanks to you in all things. Develop within them an amazingly thankful spirit. Cause them to enjoy each moment of their life, knowing that it is a gift from you. Make their hearts overflow with thankfulness to you in all they say and do, reminding them that you are the provider of all things. May your name be exalted by whatever they do today. For your glory and their good, in Jesus' name, amen.

Write down any thoughts or ideas you may want to *Share*:

Day Seven of Conduct

Father, open my eyes that I might *see* you more clearly, *savor* you more fully, and *share* you more freely.

Circle or underline any key words or phrases you *See*:

But exhort one another every day, as long as it is called "today," that none of you may be hardened by the deceitfulness of sin. (Hebrews 3:13)

Savor these truths in prayer:

Father, thank you that you do not let us just go our own way. Thank you that you care and correct us through your Word. Your correction is a demonstration of your great love for us. I pray that you would raise up friends in _____'s lives who will hold them accountable. Help them to realize that loving correction is a gift from you that helps protect them from sin. Give them the ability to spot deception and create in them eyes to see the deceitfulness of sin. Give them tender and responsive hearts when they are confronted with an area of sin in their lives. Keep them from rebelling against the people in their lives who challenge them with the truth, and protect them from hardening their hearts to that truth. For your glory and their good, in Jesus' name, amen.

Write down any thoughts or ideas you may want to *Share*:

Notes

Praying the Proverbs

Praying the Scriptures is an exhilarating exercise that God can use to expand your heart and mind for him. As you are praying for your young friend, you will find that you may need to pray about some very practical applications of The 7 Essentials. This is where I want to encourage you to pray the Proverbs. God has given us an entire book of succinct truths that bring clarity to the practical aspects of life in the Proverbs. Fresh, vibrant, real-life issues are made crisp and clear by the wisest man to step foot on earth—not including Jesus, of course. There are thirty-one chapters, so you could pray through a chapter a day if you choose. Or, you could take your time and pray through a chapter over the course of a week. For this week, I am going to take chapter three of Proverbs and demonstrate how to pray through it. Praying through the Proverbs will eventually cover each of The 7 Essentials as you work through the thirty-one chapters. May God be praised!

Day One

Father, open my eyes that I might *see* you more clearly, *savor* you more fully, and *share* you more freely.

Circle or underline any key words or phrases you *See*:

My son, do not forget my teaching, but let your heart keep my commandments, for length of days and years of life and peace they will add to you. Let not steadfast love and faithfulness forsake you; bind them around your neck; write them on the tablet of your heart. So you will find favor and good success in the sight of God and man. (Proverbs 3:1-4)

Savor these truths in prayer:

Father, I pray for _____ today, that you would bring to mind your Word and give them hearts that treasure your commands. Cause them to embrace the instruction for daily guidance, resulting in long and peace-filled lives. Help them keep your steadfast love and faithfulness in the forefront of their minds. Give them creativity in how they seek to live lives of love and faithfulness. Help them memorize and enjoy your love and faithfulness on a daily basis. Cause them to find favor and good success with you and man. Give them eyes to see your hand of favor in their lives and cause their hearts to grow big in love and faithfulness toward you and others. For your glory and their good, in Jesus' name, amen.

Write down any thoughts or ideas you may want to *Share*:

Day Two

Father, open my eyes that I might *see* you more clearly, *savor* you more fully, and *share* you more freely.

Circle or underline any key words or phrases you *See*:

Trust in the LORD with all your heart, and do not lean on your own understanding. In all your ways acknowledge him, and he will make straight your paths. Be not wise in your own eyes; fear the LORD, and turn away from evil. It will be healing to your flesh and refreshment to your bones. (Proverbs 3:5-8)

Savor these truths in prayer:

Father, thank you for your promises. Cause _____ to grow in their complete and unwavering trust in you and your promises today. Teach them to learn to trust you and keep them from leaning on their own understanding which is limited and faulty. Give them the ability to see and acknowledge your working in their lives each day. Help them trust that you will make their paths clear. Guard them against being wise in their own eyes. Cause them to fear you and turn away from even the hint of evil. Don't let them get comfortable with or delight in the slightest evil thing. Create in them a longing for holiness and righteousness that exalts you and your goodness. May you bring a wave of healing and refreshment to their bodies that would point the world to your greatness. For your glory and their good, in Jesus' name, amen.

Write down any thoughts or ideas you may want to *Share*:

Day Three

Father, open my eyes that I might *see* you more clearly, *savor* you more fully, and *share* you more freely.

Circle or underline any key words or phrases you *See*:

Honor the LORD with your wealth and with the firstfruits of all your produce; then your barns will be filled with plenty, and your vats will be bursting with wine. My son, do not despise the LORD's discipline or be weary of his reproof, for the LORD reproves him whom he loves, as a father the son in whom he delights. (Proverbs 3:9-12)

Savor these truths in prayer:

Father, I praise you as the provider of all things. I pray for _____, that you would cause their hearts to grow big for you today. Help them to see you as you are, great and glorious. Give them uncontainable pleasure in honoring you with their words, actions, and the wealth that you have provided. Give them hearts that find great joy in being very generous. Help them to know that their hope lies in you, not how much money they have in the bank. Your promises are true and you have made it clear throughout your Word that you will take care of them, as they trust you. Remind them that any season of discipline they receive from you is a sign of your absolute love for them. For your glory and their good, in Jesus' name, amen.

Write down any thoughts or ideas you may want to *Share*:

Day Four

Father, open my eyes that I might *see* you more clearly, *savor* you more fully, and *share* you more freely.

Circle or underline any key words or phrases you *See*:

Blessed is the one who finds wisdom, and the one who gets understanding, for the gain from her is better than gain from silver and her profit better than gold. She is more precious than jewels, and nothing you desire can compare with her. Long life is in her right hand; in her left hand are riches and honor. Her ways are ways of pleasantness, and all her paths are peace. She is a tree of life to those who lay hold of her; those who hold her fast are called blessed. (Proverbs 3:13-18)

Savor these truths in prayer:

Father, I pray for _____ today, that they would know the blessing of finding wisdom and understanding. Give them strong desires for you even as children, which propel them toward seeking wisdom and understanding. Give them taste buds so they may savor the treasures of a life that are found in your magnificent wisdom and understanding. May long life, riches, honor, and great joy be theirs as they follow your path of wisdom leading to peace and pleasantness. Cause their paths to lead to the tree of life, most specifically to the cross of Christ. It was your wisdom that made life possible in Jesus. Cause their hearts to pursue your wisdom above all else. For your glory and their good, in Jesus' name, amen.

Write down any thoughts or ideas you may want to *Share*:

Day Five

Father, open my eyes that I might *see* you more clearly, *savor* you more fully, and *share* you more freely.

Circle or underline any key words or phrases you *See*:

The LORD by wisdom founded the earth; by understanding he established the heavens; by his knowledge the deeps broke open, and the clouds drop down the dew. My son, do not lose sight of these—keep sound wisdom and discretion, and they will be life for your soul and adornment for your neck. Then you will walk on your way securely, and your foot will not stumble. If you lie down, you will not be afraid; when you lie down, your sleep will be sweet. (Proverbs 3:19-24)

Savor these truths in prayer:

Father, it is by your wisdom that the earth was founded and the heavens established, and for that we praise your name. I pray that _____ would see the goodness of your provision in all of creation. Cause them to learn to savor the greatness of your wisdom as they touch a blade of grass or see the stars above. May their hearts be encouraged by your sovereignty every time a raindrop splashes on their faces. Make them tenacious in seeing the preciousness of sound wisdom and discretion in everyday life. Surround them with people who walk in your wisdom and whose lives bear the fruit of your favor. Give them security, stability, peace, and sweetness of sleep because of it. For your glory and their good, in Jesus' name, amen.

Write down any thoughts or ideas you may want to *Share*:

Day Six

Father, open my eyes that I might *see* you more clearly, *savor* you more fully, and *share* you more freely.

Circle or underline any key words or phrases you *See*:

Do not be afraid of sudden terror or of the ruin of the wicked, when it comes, for the LORD will be your confidence and will keep your foot from being caught. Do not withhold good from those to whom it is due, when it is in your power to do it. Do not say to your neighbor, "Go, and come again, tomorrow I will give it"—when you have it with you. (Proverbs 3:25-28)

Savor these truths in prayer:

Father, I pray for _____ today, that they would not be fearful when bad things happen in the world. Give them a resilient confidence in you as their great Savior and Lord even now as they are young. May their peaceful confidence in you cause their peers to look to you as their hope as well. Cause them to live life with a loose grip on material things and a firm hold on you. Make them generous with their lives and resources, blessing others when it is in their power to do so. Create in them a desire and devotion to helping others in their everyday lives. Create in them an urgency to do good when they can. For your glory and their good, in Jesus' name, amen.

Write down any thoughts or ideas you may want to *Share*:

Day Seven

Father, open my eyes that I might *see* you more clearly, *savor* you more fully, and *share* you more freely.

Circle or underline any key words or phrases you *See*:

Do not plan evil against your neighbor, who dwells trustingly beside you. Do not contend with a man for no reason, when he has done you no harm. Do not envy a man of violence and do not choose any of his ways, for the devious person is an abomination to the LORD, but the upright are in his confidence. The LORD's curse is on the house of the wicked, but he blesses the dwelling of the righteous. Toward the scorners he is scornful, but to the humble he gives favor. The wise will inherit honor, but fools get disgrace. (Proverbs 3:29-35)

Savor these truths in prayer:

Father, all your ways are good and those who walk in your wisdom will inherit honor. I pray that _____ will walk humbly in your wisdom so they may know the sweetness of your favor and honor. Keep them from ever planning harm against others and help them stop others from doing so too. Give them the desire and courage to be peacemakers in their relationships. Open their eyes to see when they are becoming contentious and give them grace to turn quickly away from that path. Remind them that the devious are always at odds with you and will never receive your blessing, but those who walk uprightly will know the depth of your favor and goodness. For your glory and their good, in Jesus' name, amen.

Write down any thoughts or ideas you may want to *Share*:

Notes

WEEK THIRTEEN

Leverage Prayers

A leverage prayer is a Scripture passage that displays a prayer and effect framework. This definition may never find its way into Webster's, but it provides us with clarity as we use Scripture to pray powerfully and effectively. Leverage prayers can be identified by transitional phrases like "so that," "that you may," and "so as to." These phrases create a bridge from the prayer to the benefits of praying it. Leverage prayers are gifts from God to help us understand what can happen when we pray for specific things. Use the S3 process to make the most of these leverage prayers:

1. *See*: Identify the key components of the prayer and the benefits of the "so that" section in each prayer.

2. *Savor*: Make these prayers your own. Hover over key portions that God causes to resonate with you, and savor it in prayer for a season.

3. *Share*: Be intentional about sharing the greatness of God you are seeing and savoring in prayer with those God brings into your life.

Day One

Father, open my eyes that I might *see* you more clearly, *savor* you more fully, and *share* you more freely.

For this reason, because I have heard of your faith in the Lord Jesus and your love toward all the saints, I do not cease to give thanks for you, remembering you in my prayers, that the God of our Lord Jesus Christ, the Father of glory, may give you the Spirit of wisdom and of revelation in the knowledge of him, having the eyes of your hearts enlightened, **that you may** *know what is the hope to which he has called you, what are the riches of his glorious inheritance in the saints, and what is the immeasurable greatness of his power toward us who believe, according to the working of his great might that he worked in Christ when he raised him from the dead and seated him at his right hand in the heavenly places, far above all rule and authority and power and dominion, and above every name that is named, not only in this age but also in the one to come. And he put all things under his feet and gave him as head over all things to the church, which is his body, the fullness of him who fills all in all. (Ephesians 1:15-23)*

Prayer:

Benefits of the prayer:

Day Two

Father, open my eyes that I might *see* you more clearly, *savor* you more fully, and *share* you more freely.

For this reason I bow my knees before the Father, from whom every family in heaven and on earth is named, that according to the riches of his glory he may grant you to be strengthened with power through his Spirit in your inner being, so that Christ may dwell in your hearts through faith—that you, being rooted and grounded in love, may have strength to comprehend with all the saints what is the breadth and length and height and depth, and to know the love of Christ that surpasses knowledge, that you may be filled with all the fullness of God. (Ephesians 3:14-19)

Prayer:

Benefits of the prayer:

Day Three

Father, open my eyes that I might *see* you more clearly, *savor* you more fully, and *share* you more freely.

And it is my prayer that your love may abound more and more, with knowledge and all discernment, **so that you may** *approve what is excellent, and so be pure and blameless for the day of Christ, filled with the fruit of righteousness that comes through Jesus Christ, to the glory and praise of God. (Philippians 1:9-11)*

Prayer:

Benefits of the prayer:

Day Four

Father, open my eyes that I might *see* you more clearly, *savor* you more fully, and *share* you more freely.

*And so, from the day we heard, we have not ceased to pray for you, asking that you may be filled with the knowledge of his will in all spiritual wisdom and understanding, **so as to** walk in a manner worthy of the Lord, fully pleasing to him, bearing fruit in every good work and increasing in the knowledge of God. May you be strengthened with all power, according to his glorious might, for all endurance and patience with joy, giving thanks to the Father, who has qualified you to share in the inheritance of the saints in light. (Colossians 1:9-12)*

Prayer:

Benefits of the prayer:

Day Five

Father, open my eyes that I might *see* you more clearly, *savor* you more fully, and *share* you more freely.

...and may the Lord make you increase and abound in love for one another and for all, as we do for you, **so that he may** *establish your hearts blameless in holiness before our God and Father, at the coming of our Lord Jesus with all his saints. (1 Thessalonians 3:12-13)*

Prayer:

Benefits of the prayer:

Day Six

Father, open my eyes that I might *see* you more clearly, *savor* you more fully, and *share* you more freely.

*To this end we always pray for you, that our God may make you worthy of his calling and may fulfill every resolve for good and every work of faith by his power, **so that the name of our Lord Jesus may** be glorified in you, and you in him, according to the grace of our God and the Lord Jesus Christ. (2 Thessalonians 1:11-12)*

Prayer:

Benefits of the prayer:

Day Seven

Father, open my eyes that I might *see* you more clearly, *savor* you more fully, and *share* you more freely.

Now may the God of peace who brought again from the dead our Lord Jesus, the great shepherd of the sheep, by the blood of the eternal covenant, equip you with everything good **that you may** *do his will, working in us that which is pleasing to his sight, through Jesus Christ, to whom be glory forever and ever. Amen. (Hebrews 13:20-21)*

Prayer:

Benefits of the prayer:

Notes

APPENDIX

Giving Blessings

Parenting is one of the most challenging and rewarding roles God has given us in this life, and because of this I am always looking for ways to make it more meaningful and effective. One of the ways I have learned to do this is by asking a series of simple questions. They are questions that are designed to blow away the fog that blinds us from understanding the most important aspects of any given situation. One of these parenting questions is: *As a parent, what would you say are the top three strategies you use to help your children grow spiritually?*

I usually follow this question up with another that would seek to help parents rank the importance of the three top ways. The value of these questions is layered. These questions help parents analyze their approach to nurturing their children spiritually and to reveal possible gaps that need to be addressed in their methodology. So what about you? What would you say are the top three strategies you use to help your children grow spiritually? How would you rank your top three strategies in value and importance? What approach is number one on your list?

As a parent, I have pondered these questions for many years. For me, the questions above are designed to help us as parents to understand the primary ways we are fulfilling our calling to help our children love God with their entire beings. (Matthew 22:37-40)

I realize that parenting for your child's spiritual growth is far more complex than can be summed up in a list of three strategies. All of the forces of the world, the flesh, and the devil are intense and substantial. I also realize that there are some strategies by God's grace that can provide a far greater impact than we ever imagined. There are also good strategies that when implemented poorly can create unintended negative outcomes that can work against our spiritual goals for our children. Some of these negatives could be avoided if we spent a little more time thinking about the "what" and "whys" of our core parenting strategies.

So what's *my* number one strategy for my children's spiritual growth? Giving daily blessings to my children throughout their childhood and teen years. I believe that giving our children blessings throughout their childhood may be the most important bonding, nurturing, and soul-strengthening thing we can ever do for them.

The Act of Giving Blessing Originates with God

To receive the blessing of God is to receive the favor of God to flourish in some way. We can see this from the earliest recorded blessings in the Bible:

> *So God created man in his own image, in the image of God*
> *he created him; male and female he created them. And God*
> *blessed them. And God said to them, "Be fruitful and multi-*
> *ply and fill the earth and subdue it, and have dominion over*

the fish of the sea and over the birds of the heavens and over every living thing that moves on the earth." (Genesis 1:27-28)

And God blessed Noah and his sons and said to them, "Be fruitful and multiply and fill the earth..." (Genesis 9:1)

(Speaking to Abram who became Abraham) *"...I will bless those who bless you, and him who dishonors you I will curse, and in you all the families of the earth shall be blessed." (Genesis 12:3)*

The Bible is full of passages that reveal God's intention to show his people favor and to help them flourish. One of the most famous of all blessings recorded in the Bible is found in Numbers 6:24-27. This particular blessing was the official blessing that the Lord commanded Moses to have Aaron and the priests say over the people of Israel:

"... The LORD bless you and keep you; The LORD make his face to shine upon you and be gracious to you; The LORD lift up his countenance upon you and give you peace." So shall they put my name upon the people of Israel, and I will bless them."

Take note that this blessing is a command of God. Giving this blessing was not an option for the priests. It was a core part of their job description. God intended this blessing to be a primary source of bringing his goodness and favor to his people. Check out the culminating verse that immediately follows these three statements of blessing. Verse 27 gives us the behind the scenes intention of God in commanding this blessing to be pronounced over the nation of Israel: "So shall they put my name upon the people of

Israel, and I will bless them." *Wow!* Slow down and let this soak in. When the spiritual authorities proclaimed this God-commanded blessing over the people of Israel, they were actually placing the all-encompassing name of the Lord of the universe upon them. This is really a big deal. God himself is doing something powerful through those in spiritual authority when they pronounce this blessing over his people.

Do you realize that God has given spiritual authority not only to pastors and elders in the church but also to you as parents and grandparents? It's true, he has! Therefore, God is also doing something powerful through us when we pronounce and pray blessings over our children and grandchildren. It is simply amazing that God has established us to invite the riches of his goodness on our children by giving them blessings as he has instructed us. Are you beginning to get a glimpse of why this is my number one strategy for nurturing my children's spiritual growth?

Giving blessings may be a new or foreign idea for you right now, but stay with me and in the next few pages I will share why it has become such a treasured part of my parenting approach. I will try to give you a taste of the goodness that comes from God through the act of "giving a blessing" in my own life.

The Beginnings of Blessing

It was 1993 and my wife was living large, literally, as a woman pregnant with twin girls. I remember those days well as my bride spent over half of the pregnancy on bed rest because of premature contractions. Like most soon to be parents, we were doing everything we knew to prepare to be the best parents we could. In the process of our preparation we came across two books that shaped our understanding of the importance of giving blessings to our children. The first book was Gary Smalley and John Trent's classic book on the subject called *The Blessing*. I read it back in my seminary days, but now it was taking on a whole new significance. This book was foundational in my desire to bless our children whenever they came along. However, it was Rolf Garborg's book "The Family Blessing" that actually sealed the deal concerning this parental provision for my bride and me. In his book, Garborg shares about the biblical practice of giving blessings to your children.

As I look back on those early days as a parent, I had a lot of unspoken fear that intermingled with an overwhelming sense of joy in the approaching arrival of our daughters. As a newbie parent, who by God's grace had tasted and seen some of the goodness of God, I was determined to help my daughters have access to the sweetness of seeing, savoring, and sharing the greatness of Jesus Christ from the earliest stages of their lives. It became apparent that there was so much that I felt unprepared for as a parent and I knew that I was going to have to focus on a few vital actions that would influence the rest of my parenting. I needed to leverage some powerful principles that would have a ripple effect of goodness on my daughters. We began implementing simple acts like placing our hand on their head and asking God to bless them with his goodness in ways that only he could. Thus giving our daughters blessings became a core parenting activity.

In "The Family Blessing" Garborg spoke of how he and his wife would give blessings to their children every day from their earliest days as children. Here is where the idea of giving blessings took hold of my heart and has never let go: Garborg said that even as his children moved into their late teens they would come to him and his wife to receive their blessings each night. Even when they were away from home they would call home to receive their blessings. It did not take much for me to know in my heart that I wanted that kind of spiritual bond with my daughters from the moment they were born.

So, How Does it Work?

Giving blessings to your children is both simple and profound all at the same time. As we saw from Numbers 6:24-27, the blessing can be spoken over a group by a spiritual authority. Pastors in many churches do this every week at the end of a worship service. On a personal level when you are blessing an individual child it is an intentional moment of simple prayer and truth being spoken over them as you lift them to the Lord.

What you say and how you go about the process of giving your children blessings can vary, but be confident that the benefits for your child in receiving blessings will endure. As I think about the aspects that are involved in giving a biblical blessing to my daughters I have taken my cues from some of the patriarchs in the Old Testament and from Jesus in the gospels. Here is a beautiful example of Jacob (or Israel) as a grandparent giving blessings to Joseph's sons in Genesis 48:9-10:

> *Joseph said to his father, "They are my sons, whom God has given me here." And he said, "Bring them to me, please, that I may bless them." Now the eyes of Israel were dim with age, so that he could not see. So Joseph brought them near him, and he kissed them and embraced them.*

Giving blessings is a close personal experience. Jacob wanted his grandsons close to him and when they came close "he kissed them and embraced them."

And Israel stretched out his right hand and laid it on the head of Ephraim, who was the younger, and his left hand on the head of Manasseh, crossing his hands (for Manasseh was the firstborn). (Genesis 48:14)

Jacob placed his hands on their heads and then pronounced a blessing that was specific to these two boys.

*And he blessed Joseph and said, "The God before whom my fathers Abraham and Isaac walked, the God who has been my shepherd all my life long to this day, the angel who has redeemed me from all evil, bless the boys; and in them let my name be carried on, and the name of my fathers Abraham and Isaac; and let them grow into a multitude in the midst of the earth." * (Genesis 48:15-16)

Then in the New Testament Jesus shows us how it is done even in a culture where children were commonly undervalued.

...And they were bringing children to him that he might touch them, and the disciples rebuked them. But when Jesus saw it, he was indignant and said to them, "Let the children come to me; do not hinder them, for to such belongs the kingdom of God. Truly, I say to you, whoever does not receive the kingdom of God like a child shall not enter it." And he took them in his arms and blessed them, laying his hands on them. (Mark 10:13-16)

As you can see it is a very simple and straightforward gift to a child. I like what Rob Rienow says in his book, *Visionary Parenting*: "When parents regularly speak blessings to their children it increases their sense of peace and safety."

Early Beginnings

In our family, the blessings we prayed over our daughters had the tendency to take on the flavor of the specific life stage they were in at the time. When our daughters were babies we would sing their blessings to them. Michael Card had a "Lullaby" album that had the words to the Numbers 6:24-26 blessing put to music. This song made it easy to hold them and gently sing these words of blessing over them. Admittedly it was more soothing when my wife sang to them but they still seemed to be comforted when I blessed them in this way.

As they became a little older we would place our hand on their heads and alternate between singing and speaking the blessing over them as they lay in their beds. Gradually, we transitioned to just speaking the blessing over them with our hand resting on their heads.

"No, no daddy, look at me!"

Parenting toddlers always provides for excitement, surprise, and sometimes some treasured insight. I remember one time when I was giving my daughter Bethany her blessing and I closed my eyes and began the blessing. I had only said a few words when I heard her say, "No, no daddy, look at me!" She wanted to see me look at her as I spoke the blessing over her. She was my teacher that night on how to upgrade the benefit of giving a blessing. Up to that point I might have my eyes open or closed with no real rhyme or reason, but not after that. My daughter taught me the importance of intentional eye contact.

Elementary Age

What if my kids are already in elementary school? Is it too late to start? Absolutely not! It is never too late to start lavishing your children with blessings. You will just need to do a little groundwork because this will be new for your children. **Honesty is the best policy.** I have found that it works best to introduce the idea as something you have recently come across in a book you were reading and were encouraged by an idea you wanted to begin implementing into your family. Explain to them how it will go down. Help them know what to expect. Tell them that you will place your hand on their head and look them in the eye and say the blessing. Tell them you may even read the blessing from Numbers 6 as your starting point. Several things will influence how you begin:

- **How many children are in your family?** If you have one child you will be able to introduce the concept in a casual way in the normal walking patterns of your life. If you have multiple children it would probably be best to consider having some sort of family meeting.

- **Is prayer a normal part of the everyday rhythm of your family?** For example, do you pray at meals or have prayer for family members or friends who are sick? If so this will provide a context where introducing the idea will not be completely new to them.

- **Do you have any type of family devotions?** If you do you may want to introduce the idea by looking at the story of Jacob blessing his grandchildren or Jesus blessing the children that were brought to him.

- **Do you tuck your children in at night?** That could be a great time to start giving them blessings. If you don't, is there a time that is natural for you to begin giving blessings?

During the elementary ages of our girls we would spend time as a family reading missionary biographies from a series by Youth With A Mission or YWAM for short. These were incredible times when we would be temporarily transported to India with Ida Scudder, the great medical missionary, or to Africa with Mary Slessor of Calabar. My wife and I had made a commitment to have a family time of devotions with our girls in a way that suited their age. When they were younger we used a resource from Desiring God for children that had key stories from the Old and New Testaments with a corresponding coloring book. I would read the story and they would color the picture and tell us about the story. As they got older we shifted to the missionary biographies. When they entered middle and high school we tended to read a chapter from the proverbs or another book of the Bible alternating with great Christian books. Our family devotions together had a powerful influence on the content of my blessing for my daughters that evening. For example if we were reading about Mary Slessor of Calabar in family devotions I would probably give a blessing that reflected that.

> *The Lord bless you and keep you, Abby and Bethany. The LORD make his face shine upon you and give you peace. May the LORD give you courage, compassion, and tenacious faith like Mary Slessor of Calabar. In the name of the Father, Son, and Holy Spirit. Amen.*

My goal was for my daughters to not only be inspired by the lives of these great missionaries, but also to sense that God has his hand on their lives as well. I have also found that it's important to make the blessing personal. It doesn't take much to do so, but it does make a difference. You can always add more to the ending of the blessing depending on the needs of the child you are blessing at that moment. But remember, asking for God's blessing is no small thing. Having the security, favor, and peace of God flowing toward you is foundational to life!

Coming Full Circle

It's been over two decades since God inspired my wife and me with Rolf Garborg's book *The Family Blessing*. In that time, my daughters have received over 12,000 blessings each (and that is being conservative!) My daughters seemed to be on the fast track to becoming blessing-saturated children since they received blessings from both parents daily and twice a day during the early elementary years of school; once as they went off to school and another as they went to bed each evening. I am amazed and thankful for this extraordinary number of blessings. This simple parenting act has proved to be more of a blessing to our whole family than I ever imagined.

When my daughters were about three years old we were visiting my dad and stepmother. We always enjoyed visiting them over the years. My dad loved my daughters and enjoyed having them around. On this particular trip my daughter Abby decided in her take-charge three-year-old way that Paw Paw and Granny Ann should join us for our family devotions. Abby was unaware that they did not embrace our hope in Jesus, but was able to persuade them to join us. They didn't know that joining us meant that they would also be given prayer requests to pray for as well. God was gracious in using a child to open the way to share the sweetness of knowing Jesus in our devotions time. The night was concluded by Abby approaching my father to give him a blessing. My dad was sitting on a bar stool when she came to do her deed. I remember my dad turning to me with a puzzling look on his face, asking me what Abby wanted. I told him that I thought she wanted to give him a blessing and that all he need to do was lean over and she would take care of the rest. That moment is still clear in my mind with my dad leaning over and my three year old daughter reaching up with her hand on his head, gently uttering the words "The LORD bless you and keep you and make his face shine upon you and give you peace. In the name of the Father, Son, and Holy Spirit. Amen". I never imagined that incorporating giving blessings to my daughters would have blessed my unbelieving father. The blessings of God's grace always seem to spill over onto others.

For my daughters' junior years of college, they had to travel to school for the beginning of the semester at different times because one of them had to report early for her Resident Assistant (RA) responsibilities. When you translate that, it means I had the opportunity to make the 12-hour round trip to their college two times in a two-week period. On my second journey I had successfully delivered my non-RA daughter to school and was readying myself for the 6-hour trek home. I had made my rounds saying goodbye and was about to leave when one of my daughters called out for me to wait as she came up to the car. What happened next confirmed to me that giving blessings to my children is the most powerful parenting tool ever invented by our heavenly Father. She looked at me through the open car door window and proceeded to reach in through the window placing her hand on my head and gave me a blessing. The goodness of the family blessing had come full circle in that moment. That brief but lingering moment immediately entered my top ten list of greatest parenting moments! I hope and pray that these few pages have convinced you to make giving your children or grandchildren blessings a key part of your parenting strategies for nurturing your children spiritually, emotionally, and relationally.

A Special Note to Parents

Dear Parent,

You are the most influential person in your child's life. God has ordained your role of influence and blessing for your children. Use this book to expand and deepen your influence in the ways that you invest in your children spiritually. The Pray for Me Campaign is designed to empower you to build a network of spiritual care and support for your children. Make inviting three adults from three generations to be your children's Prayer Champions a natural part of your life. Here are some things to remember and consider as you move forward.

- It will be easiest to do this when your church has made the PFMC a part of how they are encouraging and supporting children and families.
- There is no need for you to delay securing Prayer Champions for your children if the timing is not right for your church as a whole to launch the PFMC.
- Talk to your children about who they would like to invite to be their Prayer Champions.
- Helping your children learn to invite adults to be their Prayer Champions equips them to flourish. The adults

who become their Prayer Champions will desire to see them succeed in faith and life.

- Consider sending an email to potential Prayer Champions letting them know what you and your family are doing and your children's interest in having them as one of their Prayer Champions.
- Empower the Prayer Champions to pray well for your children by providing them this Prayer Guide.
- Take special note of the section on Giving Blessings. Begin the practice of giving your children blessings to give them a very real sense of your love and God's care for them.

It is my prayer that the Lord would lavish you with an abundance of his favor and wisdom for every aspect of your role as a parent.

Lastly, we would love to hear from you. Share a story, a word of encouragement or anything else that would help us serve you and other parents well.

For the Glory of God and the good of every child,

Tony Souder

Founder, Pray for Me Campaign

What's Next?

Take the next step and become a Movement Champion today. A Movement Champion is a supporter of the Pray for Me Campaign who does three simple things:

1. **Pray.** Movement Champions pray for the advancement of the Campaign.
2. **Share.** Movement Champions spread the word about the Campaign.
3. **Give.** Movement Champions give at least $10/month to the Campaign.

Your role helps bring the greatness of God to the next generation and makes the difference in students' lives. Become a Movement Champion today!

www.prayformecampaign.com/give

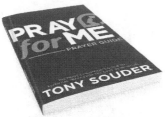